George R. Pembroke

Roots, a Plea for Tolerance

George R. Pembroke

Roots, a Plea for Tolerance

ISBN/EAN: 9783743423046

Manufactured in Europe, USA, Canada, Australia, Japa

Cover: Foto ©ninafisch / pixelio.de

Manufactured and distributed by brebook publishing software (www.brebook.com)

George R. Pembroke

Roots, a Plea for Tolerance

ROOTS

A PLEA FOR TOLERANCE

ROOTS

A PLEA FOR TOLERANCE

A NEW EDITION

LONDON
RICHARD BENTLEY & SON, NEW BURLINGTON STREET
Publishers in Ordinary to Her Majesty the Queen
1888

PREFACE

My old man has told me that I am a fool for publishing these sketches; and when he commits himself to such an opinion, there is generally, at least, a half truth in it.

But I have learnt some lessons from the thoughts I have tried to express in them, why should not other people? And, unless I am much mistaken, the reader can deduce almost any moral from them he pleases, according to the bias of his mind—that religion is essential and free-thinking useless, religion pleasant and free-thinking terrible — that utility and absolute truth should be looked upon as separate—that they should not—that thinking is but an idle waste of thought, and all is everything and everything is nought—that a sceptic is not necessarily the child of the devil—that the subject is so large, and so impossible for any really deep thinker to simplify and settle, that we should not be too hasty in condemning our neighbours for disagreeing with us—that my young friend was a prig—that I am a fool—and half-a-dozen more, all calculated, as the poor boy would have said, to do good in various and perhaps contrary directions.

There is one defect in them which I am anxious to confess and apologise for; that is, the apparent disregard of the accurate meanings of words. It is a stumbling-block that has been the cause of much misunderstanding even of the most careful and learned writers. To an unphilosophical person like myself the difficulty is almost hopeless, and I have been forced to attempt exactness by inexactness; that is, by giving the same idea under several different verbal forms. I think in this I have been partially successful, and that any one who wishes to understand these conversations will not have much difficulty in doing so; while those who wish to misunderstand and misrepresent them are welcome to that pleasure.

But the reader must pardon me for not seeing the weaknesses of my work as plainly as he does; for when I am reading it, the awkward phraseology, the general rawness of composition, fade away before my eyes, and the rude drawing merges itself into the living pictures I knew and loved so well.

And to-day, of all others, I feel my critical powers lulled to sleep.

For we had buried him as he wished, on the very verge of the cliff of Farewell Point, on the spot where he and Mary and I had spent so many happy hours. For he had said half laughing, that he should not like to lie in a strange haunt; that, however silly and heathenish it might seem, he liked the idea of the fresh, cool, southern breeze, that had wafted him so pleasantly to the happy islands in the tropics, singing through the trees over his grave, with the growl of the surf for ever in his ears; with the kahawai frolicking in the sea close beneath, and the great sulky Stingarees floating about in the still water amongst the rocks, and the terns and the gannets swooping and screaming all round.

So we did as he wished; and my old man and I wanted to put up a stone and an inscription to his memory; but Mary, in her quiet, determined way, begged us to leave that to her, and to-day she took me up to see what she had done.

And with our feet in the soft waving grass, with the warm north wind singing in our ears, we stood for a long time silent, hand in hand, gazing with dim eyes at a rude tablet let into the trunk of the great tree, on which was written—

'BE HONEST: FEAR NOTHING: TRUST GOD.'

ROOTS

CHAPTER I

'Why on earth are good people so unbearable to live with?' cry I, throwing myself down on the grass, regardless of damp, rheumatism, and a new dress. 'Why can't they let me go on in my natural way in and out of scrapes of all kinds? *I* know I should come out of them all right, but they haven't the slightest conception of the hundred-and-one feelings that would make me go straight, and only grudge me the liberty that they themselves are afraid of. What is goodness? They are good; I think I am too, in a way. I know you are; and yet I heard one of them, who had sat next to you at dinner on some occasion, declare that you had an utter absence of all principles of religion and morality, and ought not to be admitted into any Christian society.'

My philosophical young friend turns lazily

over on to his elbows, blows a cloud of tobacco-smoke out of his mouth, looks wistfully into the distance for about one minute, and then gives forth the text of his discourse in these words: 'Machine-made good people can't understand that unmachine-made goodness can exist—can't even understand goodness being made by any machine but the one that made theirs.' I have the faintest glimmering of what he means, but say nothing. 'My idea is,' he continues, 'that religions are virtue-making machines, using terrorism or temptations, as the case may be, to make people do what they should do naturally, and would do if they were perfect—which they ain't. Now, there are two sets of good people in this world: the ones who are made good by the machinery of a religious theory that they believe implicitly, and another who do good actions naturally, without much *arrière pensée* about their duty. Of course there is a third set, who combine the two, and these are the best of all, but we have nothing to do with them at present. I don't want to disparage the first set at all; as far as my human mind can judge, I should be inclined to think that the man who does what he thinks right, whether he likes it or not, from a sense of duty, is more worthy in the sight of his Maker than the man who does right naturally, because it is part of his nature to worship good and noble things; but though the Pharisee (if he be not a hypocrite) may be the best man of the two, there is no doubt that the Publican is the most lovable.'

'But surely,' cry I, 'you can't call a man who naturally worships good and noble things a "Publican?"'

'I'm afraid,' answers he, rather sadly, 'that they often are both Publicans and sinners; ay, the very best of them, like Charles Kingsley's Lancelot in *Yeast*, who, to my mind, is one of the finest, truest characters ever drawn.'

'But you, though you have rather discarded the "virtue-making machines," as you call them haven't become like that,' say I, letting out what first came into my head in my usual incorrigible fashion.

'Perhaps simply because I have not got a redundance of animal nature and lots of head development at the back below the ears,' answered he laughing. 'It's just possible that if I had, a machine might be my only chance. But to go back to our subject. The good people you speak of, who are, as I said before, made good by a particular machine, can't understand goodness existing apart from it. The machine-made missionary finds good in the heathens he has come to convert, and wonders vaguely how it got there, or makes astounding theories concerning God and man, to account for it. They fancy they have got a patent for God's light. Because their means are different from yours and mine, they jump to the conclusion that our ends are different likewise, and that we must necessarily be extraordinarily miserable sinners.'

'Well, that partly accounts for their not understanding me, but not for my not appreciating them. Somehow, many of their best and kindest actions give me a cold shiver of ungraciousness.'

'Because their self-consciousness, their *arrière pensée* of duty take all the flavour out of the good action to our poor human palates. It's very unfair on them, perhaps, but so it is. Supposing a man does you some very kind turn. If you imagine that he has done it spontaneously, out of affection or simple goodness of heart, you feel intensely grateful. If you know that he has helped you merely because it was his religious duty to do so, you feel very ungracious, and hear, perhaps, a little devil whispering in your ear that the interests of his own dirty soul had something to do with it. Then, again, you feel you can't trust them as you can those spontaneous sinners. You have to depend, not on their hearts, but on their consciences. If I were in a bad scrape or trouble, my scapegrace friend —— would help me to the death without thinking why; my good friend ——, who, as you know, is the *best* man in our parts, and gives away as much as ever he can spare, would very likely either find an excuse to his conscience for leaving me alone, or help me in such a way as would compel me to kick him out of the house.'

'And you think this last man better than the first?' say I.

'Strictly speaking, I suppose he is; but I say simply that the other is the most lovable. The world in general agrees with me, if it would only own it. There is more real human nature in that commonplace defence, "He is such a good-hearted fellow, I can't help being fond of him," than people often think. Corporal Trim (I think it was) hit the truth when he answered the nurse who said she tended him for the love of God by saying he had much rather she had done it for the love of him. And men are so sharp at finding out motives. You see two good clergymen in some horrible district full of poverty, and the sin and misery that follow in its train. Both work equally hard, are equally clever (we'll suppose), yet one is worshipped and welcomed everywhere, and so can do good, the other makes no way at all. Depend on it you will find the latter a machine-made good man, and the former a spontaneously good-hearted one, seldom thinking of his duty or his salvation either.

'I'll tell you a true story, but can't give you the real names. There was once three young fellows at college together, we'll call them Smith, Brown, and Thompson. Different as they were in character, they had been close friends ever since their nursery days. Smith was very good, religious almost to unwholesomeness. Brown, a merry, rather thoughtless, young scapegrace, with a thoroughly good heart. Thompson, by far the cleverest and the most charming, poor fellow, of the three. They went their different ways into the world.

'I needn't tell you how poor Thompson went to the dogs. It was one of those utter shipwrecks at the beginning of life, caused more by inexperience than wickedness, that are so sad and seem so unfair. He disappeared, as such men do. Some years after Smith called on Brown and told him that he had heard by chance that Thompson, worn out by drink, and worse, was dying in some wretched hole, and he thought it his duty to go and see if he could do anything for him. They set off together at once, and walked in silence, Smith, I suspect, thinking about his duty towards his neighbour, shuddering at the thought of poor Thompson's wickedness, trying to nerve himself up, poor fellow, for the scene he had to face. What Brown thought of I don't think he could tell you exactly, his mind was in a whirl. Old school and college scenes, when he and Thompson had been chums together, kept flitting swiftly through his brain, and every now and then the unanswerable question, "Why him and not me? He was as good, nay, had more good in him than I had to start with. The consequences of one sin broke him for life!" Brown wasn't given to reflection, and it was little wonder that such a question confused him completely. At last they reached their destination in one of those filthy slums which few but the clergyman, the doctor, and the policeman are unfortunate enough to know the existence of; and after conciliating a most disreputable-looking old woman by means of half-a-crown, were shown into a room so filthy and comfortless that I will leave the description of it to your imagination. There lay Thompson, dying, wasted, disfigured, frightfully changed, but recognisable still. He looked up as they entered, knew them at once (poor fellow! he wasn't likely to forget *their* face in his five years of hell), and said weakly, "How good of you fellows to come! I am afraid I can't offer you a chair." Smith, good man, had never felt so miserable before. Often, in his work as a clergyman, he had seen much what he saw then, but had never realised it in the same way. They had been friends once, and now there seemed (don't judge him too harshly) such an impassable gulf between him and the dying sinner. He thought of his duty— tried to stammer out a few of the religious commonplaces that usually came so glibly, but was stopped by "My dear Smith, I have made my bed and must lie on it; but I don't want to end my life arguing with you or myself, having had enough of that torture every night for years past. Brown, old fellow, are you never going to speak to me?" Brown had been standing silent, trembling, since they entered the room.

'For an instant the question that had been haunting him flashed across his brain, then came a deep wondering awe, till all was swallowed by a wild yearning love for his old friend. It never occurred to *him* that there was a gulf between them—that Thompson was a greater sinner than himself; he knelt down beside the wretched pallet, took one of the poor wasted hands in his, and bending over it, cried like a great baby.'

'What was the end?' ask I, after a long pause, during which I have been struggling with a certain lumpy feeling about the throat, produced solely, so catching are these things, by a decided huskiness in my young friend's voice.

'They tried to nourish him, but it was too late, and so for about three hours he lay peacefully and silently, holding Brown's hand, and smiling as he listened to the prattle of old days, till at last he looked up with such an expression of love as I have never seen before or since in a face, said simply, "Dear old boy," and died.'

'Rather a heathen deathbed.'

'I am not so sure of that. If, as you Christians hold, "God is love," I fancy he was nearer to Him in those last hours than he ever was in his life.'

I murmur something about 'preparing to meet his God.'

'Humph,' answers he. 'You would have been a clever woman if you could have persuaded Thompson that prayers or wishes uttered in his last moments would change God's opinion about his life. He would tell you that he thought such an idea not only absurd, but rather blasphemous, for a prayer implies a possibility of inducing God to do something. If not, why pray?'

'It is dreadful to think of the future state of a man like that.'

'You know,' answered he earnestly, 'that though I am a professed sceptic I never attack people's creeds, as a rule, because I think they do so much good. But I must depart a little from my rule now. It is your creed that makes the thought of poor Thompson's future dreadful—I could not bear to believe such dreadful things of God as you Christians profess to do. You hold that certain laws of right and wrong applicable to us human atoms are not only divine in the sense of being intended by God for us, but really to a great extent applicable to God Himself. You talk of His justice, mercy, etc., as if He was human, having made a deified man of Him, the *inevitable consequence* of trying to realise Him personally, because a perfect man is the highest thing we are able to conceive—having thus given Him, in your attempt to realise Him, ideas of right and wrong much like our own, you are forced to have some theory, however lame, to explain the cruelties of all life and nature, part of which theory is the doctrine of future rewards and punishments. Consequently you are forced to believe that millions of your fellow-creatures, after all their troubles in this life, which are bad enough in all conscience, are being punished in the next. And as you hold that God is omniscient, you are committed to the belief that He knowingly created thousands of beings with a destiny of misery. And this you call a religion of love? I tell you if I believed and realised this (which most people do not), I could not bear life.'

'It is very horrible, certainly; but it would be just as bad to believe that none of the injustices and troubles of this life would be rectified in the next.'

'Quite so.'

'What then?'

'I simply say, as I have heard clergymen do, with rather a different meaning, twenty times, these things are beyond human knowledge, and we must trust them to God. I say that I have seen every religion and many philosophies, all trying to make some theory and explanation of the terrible mysteries of nature, such as pain and trouble, and after coolly passing over a dozen plain facts to make it harmonious, all failing hopelessly, and producing some such contradictory monstrosity as the one I have mentioned. It seems to me plain that the reason of their failure is simply that God and His ways are beyond human comprehension, and must be, at least until we cease to judge God by a man's ideas; wherefore I say plainly that I know nothing about these things, believe that they are unknowable to man, and trust them to God.'

'The radical difference between you and an orthodox parson seems to me to be that you draw a different line between the knowable and the unknowable, and that your religion requires the greatest trust in God.'

'Well put,' said he; 'I think he draws the line in a wrong place. He says, here are certain facts revealed by God. I ask him where he got his first knowledge of Him to enable him to be sure of this, which of course he can't answer. Waiving that point, I say, these facts, to be any use to me, must be real living ones, with all their inevitable consequences attached, and, taken one with the other, the facts he offers me teach things so repulsive to my reverence for God that I see no other course but to confess that these things are utterly beyond human knowledge, and that therefore no one has the right to lay down the law about them.

'As far as my religion of scepticism requiring the greatest faith goes, that is evident, though not generally acknowledged.

> '" Many have *faith* enough all thought to scout,
> But few trust God enough to dare to doubt."

And though you will never hear such a thing spoken from the pulpit, I tell you that the chief reason why the best "scepticism" (as it is called) never holds its own against any religion in any country is, that men have not got faith and humility enough to bear it. They will accept the lowest theories about God, the lowest explanations about His ways —anything, anything—rather than own that He is beyond their ken. How can a religion of doubt, humility, and implicit trust ever gain a hold amongst them, while the birth of their religious wants still lies in the words, "Oh God, give me a sign that I may know that I am not utterly forsaken!" Ay! and the more signs and audacious dogmas the religion holds forth the greater are its numbers and perhaps the more good it does. And so it comes to pass that I am tolerant of opinions that I despise and detest. I deny their truth; I believe in their utility. What could I, with my creed, say to convert some poor ignorant rascal? Nothing! What inducement (to put it plainly) could I hold out to him to repent? None! How could I put my trust in God into his heart unaided by any tangible "revelation?" And so, though I believe it true and right, I believe it useless to men as they are, useless perhaps for thousands of years to come. It will grow up in men's hearts itself when they are ready for it; it *cannot* be the instrument that will make them so.

'And so, friend priest, let us be friends. Your way of thinking (whatever religion you may be of) has done incalculable good, and been the cause of every persecution in the world; mine has done but little, except to a few individual souls, and may lead to mere fatalistic indifference.'

The bitterness, but not the sadness, of his face and voice had passed away when he spoke again.

'We are all pieces of some great puzzle, and know nothing of its harmonious whole, I suppose.

Your conscience seems to speak with God's voice and tells you not to doubt ; mine does the same, and tells me that I have no right to decide on what I know nothing about. It would be bearable if you religious people weren't so apt to insist that my conscience must be a lying prophet because it disagrees with yours. . . . I may be striving for a kind of faith beyond my powers as yet, but must follow on. . . . Trust, trust ! '

And then he laid his young head wearily down in the long grass, and said no more.

And I stood up, and advancing to the extreme point of the lofty promontory on which we had been lying, gazed away over the great southern sea, studded here with innumerable rocks and islets shaped like beehives and pine-apples. The day was a glorious one ; a fresh sea-breeze whitened the tops of the countless waves. The clouds galloped joyously across the sky, mottling the bright blue sea with great patches of rich red purple, coursing on over the forest-clad hills of the mainland beyond, changing them, painting them with careless beauty. I heard the melodious notes of the *tui* and the bell-bird echoing joyfully through the glens of the island. How beautiful it all seems ! A flock of dapper little terns, black-headed, red-beaked, are making havoc among the small fry in the water below my feet, aided by a shoal of ravenous *kahawai*, who are chasing them to the surface. Is this beautiful ? I have come across my young friend's ever-present mystery—

pain, terror, destruction. Is there a devil in it all? Is all nature some mere careless, pitiless Car of Juggernaut? I am afraid I have not faith enough for his simple 'Don't know' religion, so I had better not think about it. Thank Heaven I have not got his horrible habit of realising things vividly. I see a brave little cutter coming up close-hauled, leaping furiously at the waves as she meets them, and hiding herself in clouds of spray; and as I turn to the other side of the promontory I am standing on I see almost beneath my feet a fine sleek schooner lying at anchor in the dead-calm land-locked bay, with two men apparently fast asleep on the forecastle, and I become possessed by the idea that it is some good, self-satisfied, contented, religious man, and the cutter outside my unfortunate young friend.

And then I looked at him contentedly dreamily smoking his pipe, as if everything but comfort was a fifth wheel to the waggon, and tried to reflect upon what he had been saying. Of course, though I had no answers to give him, he hasn't shaken my faith in the least. Like a great many others, I am constitutionally superior to reason on religious matters; besides, when one has arrived at middle age, and been surrounded all one's life, whether one likes it or not, by conventionality and orthodoxy, such things have become a second skin. In fact I am too old, too lazy, and perhaps too stupid, to doubt and speculate. But it floated across my mind that I had seen a glimpse of a terribly living soul, and it seemed to me somehow monstrous and horrible that such a one should be in our modern days so completely cut off from any spiritual communion from the best of his fellow-men. I wondered whether he would, influenced by those about him, gradually slide back into their ways of thought and life, and live and die nominally a good religious man, really infinitely more godless and soul-sleeping than he is now. I didn't think that possible: his spirit was too restless. Would he be driven by bitterness and loneliness (in plain words) to the devil? 'Oh!' thought I, with the conceit of my sex, 'if he could only get hold of the right woman!'

And at last I break the silence by saying a little nervously, 'Ain't people who hold your kind of opinions very apt to get bad?'

'Very,' answers he, decidedly. 'And it is the machine-made good people who unconsciously make them so. Would you like to know how it happens in most cases?

'We will suppose ten young men, about the age of nineteen, going up together to Oxford. In all probability nine of them, though looked on as awfully good fellows by their friends, and good boys by their affectionate parents, are utterly godless in every sense of the word. I mean they go to church, say their prayers, and do their duty towards their neighbour to a greater or lesser extent; but their religion is not to them a living one, they believe it as a matter of course, but never think what they believe. The articles of faith they repeat so glibly are not real vivid facts, with certain connections between them and carrying with them certain inevitable consequences. The tenth, on the other hand, has got a yeasty realising mind—the mysteries of God, life, and nature, are perpetually floating before him; everything commonplace and extraordinary must have a meaning and a connection. At college they all learn more or less history, philosophy, logic, etc., together, but the nine never apply them practically to their own convictions. Their religion (God forgive me if I speak unjustly) is too dead and too distant to be in any danger of attack. With the tenth it is different. With him every one thing seems connected with another. He doesn't know how to draw an exact line between things to be thought about and things to be left alone. Again, he is too earnest to show his religious ideas any more logical mercy than the rest; and so the chances are that he gets very grave doubts about some things he has always believed implicitly, and becomes more or less a freethinker in spite of himself for at least a year or two, not because he is worse, but because he is better and more religious than the rest. And then, if he gets among our machine-made good people, Lord help him! If they try and convert him they are out of their depth at once, because they don't know and can scarcely understand his side of the question. So they are obliged to fall back on the dogma that it is sinful to doubt on such subjects. They are shocked whenever he opens his mind or his mouth, and thus do his poor sensitive struggling soul the worst turn they can by driving it inwards. The poor wretch is struggling, in the bitter humility of doubt, after truth, and they calmly tell him that he is self-confident and conceited, and that he had better beware lest he should fall.

'I must say they do their best to foster conceit in him. They show at every turn that they simply have not thought enough on such things to understand his difficulties. Yet all of them, from the old grandfather down to the young lady of nineteen, think themselves in a position to pity his errors; while he can't help knowing that not half of them have ever examined into the truth of the things they are so certain of, not a third of them realised the real meanings, connections, and consequences of the doctrines they profess to believe. And so, when the poor wretch is sufficiently filled with a sense of utter loneliness, bitterness, and morbid vanity, his strength and trust in God give way, and he, in some form or another —goes to the devil. And they all cry with a shudder, good people, "Poor John! *I* always knew what his infidelity would lead to!" Never dreaming that they themselves are answerable for his ruin!'

'I don't see how it is to be helped, though,' say I, rather priding myself on my common-sense. 'You can't expect the world in general to be truth-seekers, in a state of suspense, to doubt the dogmas that make their lives happy, and discard all certainty in religion — without which they wouldn't see any use in it.'

'No; I don't see how it can be helped: I only say that it is a sad truth. No; though I tell the religious man with bitter truth, "You have no prior knowledge of God to justify you in being positively certain that what you call your "revelations" come from Him; it is a mere question of human judgment, and you have no more right to be positive on such matters than I have—I know that if he had not that conceit, if he did not claim that infallibility for his creed, it would be what mine is: affirming nothing, trusting everything, and consequently utterly unattractive and useless to men. "Don't know" may be true; but how can it have any good influence on men's minds? It can make them humble, perhaps, and that is all.

'That conceit—that assumption and belief in infallibility, has been the root of all the evil and all the good that religions have done in this strange world. The blood of ten thousand martyrs is on its head: the bitterness of millions of miserable lives lies at its door. I despise it for its vanity, its narrowness, its ignorance: I *hate* it for its cruelties. But this same narrow conceited assumption of possessing infallible truth supported the martyr whose death it had decreed. It was the glory of his life, the cause of his goodness; it enabled him to die and triumph in his death. It has roused and still rouses men, from being mere impulsive animals or dreaming speculators, into being earnest workers, giving them a meaning and a purpose in life. It has at least helped largely to create all the greatest of mankind; it is in fact the mainspring of that virtue-making machine called "religion;" and I, the sceptic, who despise and hate it for itself, solemnly declare to you that I believe men cannot be improved without it.

'So,' added he, after a short pause, 'we poor sceptics must bear with it. And when (whatever religion we are surrounded by) we are snubbed, hurt, and exasperated by its pig-headed conceit and narrow injustice, we should ask ourselves this question: "Could my negative truth do half as much good as I see this positive trash doing day by day?"'

'Well,' said I, laughing, 'I must do you the justice to say that you are the only person I ever met, honest enough to own that your religion was perfectly useless.'

'Useless, except to a very few isolated minds, whose over-keen nose for blasphemy makes it inconquerably disgusting to hear people laying down the law about things they believe beyond human knowledge, and who have a most extraordinary reluctance to believe in the infallible truth of their own convictions. I assure you,' he added, with a quiet laugh, 'such specimens are very rare. Our religious friends need not be so bitter against us, for I don't see the slightest chance of our stepping into their shoes, simply because we can't offer mankind any articles of the sort they want.'

And so this conversation ended, somewhat unsatisfactorily, as talks between people who have but few ideas in common generally do, and we walked home through the *kauri* forest in the deepening twilight, my young friend talking pleasantly, putting new life into old truisms, and seeing some natural meaning (*never an allegory*) in every commonplace object. I don't intend to try and give the moral of our conversation, if it had any, and I could do it. I leave that to my readers. Some, I think, would simply come to the conclusion that my young friend is a prig, a fool, or a madman. I was only conscious of feeling an increased largeness of heart and a soul refreshed by the feeling of having been freed for the time from the wearing and shallowness of everyday thoughts by going to the back of everything. I can't help it if you can't understand it. I don't know how to express my feelings better.

I don't think I need apologise for making public this conversation. To those machine-made good people who never knew doubt it *may* give a slight shock, but no hurt, as they will not know the alphabet that formed the language. Those who do know such doubts it cannot harm.

CHAPTER II

IT was a glorious evening as my young philosophical friend and I settled ourselves down for a quiet talk in the long grass on the top of Farewell Point. The sun was sinking behind the dark mountains on the mainland, sending a ten-mile path of gold across the smooth sea to the rocks beneath our feet. The last breath of air had died away, and the great Pacific was gradually sullenly heaving, till it wearied itself into a dead calm, 'Just like (said my young friend) a tempestuous woman recovering from a fit of hysterics.' Even the murmuring *pohutikawas* had ceased to wail their dirges over the sleepy water, and there was no sound but the distant growl of the long swell on some more exposed point, the note of a lively parson-bird,[1] imitating the accents of some member of his congregation with most reprehensible facetiousness, and the splash of the frivolous

[1] The *tui* is called 'the parson-bird,' partly because he has two white feathers hanging from under his throat, partly because he always has a great deal to say for himself—at least, so say irreverent woodcutters.

dancing mullet in the still harbour. Peace, calm, rest, everywhere; yet what so jarring as a scene like this when one is heavy at heart? I had got out of bed the wrong side this morning, as the nursemaids say. In the first place a cutter had arrived at daylight, bringing the news of the failure of poor Jean Haynes's run on the Kaiwarra, involving the loss of three hundred pounds my good man had lent him to start with; *consequently* my good man thought fit to find fault with my wild unsystematic way of educating the children; *consequently* (that being almost my only purpose and pleasure in life) I retorted that they were the only children I knew who looked on learning as a pleasure, *consequently* my worthy sister-in-law was set on to me, to lecture me on everything in general, and the conventionalities and the training of children in particular; *consequently*, in my desperation, I came out with a speech that would have made her hair stand on end, had it not been trained in far too orthodox a manner to dream of doing anything of the kind; *consequently* both she and my good man preached a joint sermon upon my innate wickedness; *consequently* I rushed into the bush and made my way up to Farewell Point in a very sore frame of mind. What an old fool I must be to let these continuous petty troubles make life so unbearable to me! How slow some people live! Here am I, after forty years of humdrum life amongst humdrum people, not yet able to fit myself into their groove, and still as sensitive about being misunderstood and unappreciated as a morbid child. Well, well! We people with imaginations must pay for the pleasure of dreaming, I suppose. But still it is terrible to have to force one's mind into an unnatural shape, not for a day, but for a life; to be taught constantly that all one's most innocent impulses have a sin lurking at their root; to hear that all thoughts that do not run in a certain groove are contraband. Bah! I know now what my young friend meant by saying that machine-made good people sent many of their fellow-creatures to the devil.

My young friend appeared to have guessed my thoughts to some degree, for, after looking quizzingly into my troubled face, he struck up the following remarkable doggerel :—

> 'Oh, would I were a vegetable,
>   A cabbage, or a cauliflower!
> Unconscious and unfidgetable,
>   I'd dream away life's bitterest hour.
>
> 'To stop my thinking, I would be
>   A demmed, cold, damp unpleasant body;
> I'd be a monk, I'd be a she,
>   I'd swamp my brains in whisky-toddy.
>
> 'Oh, theirs must be a happy life,
>   To have no brains or botheration,
> And when the time comes for the knife,
>   Be ate with placid resignation.
>
> 'Their gentle state my——'

'Where on earth does that nonsense come from?' interrupted I, crossly.

'That nonsense,' replied he, gravely, 'was written by me some years ago, at a time when I had so addled my poor little brains with speculating that I was beginning to prepare myself for suicide or madness. The verses themselves will tell you what a state of despairing idiocy I was reduced to. It was just at the time when I was entering upon my present phase, and hadn't got accustomed to its worries.'

'What phase do you call that?'

'Well, I don't know a name for it in English, for we English always affect to be rather ashamed of it; but the Germans call it something that sounds like *Sturm und Drang*. It is a disease arising from a sudden increase in the vitality of the spirit, which is apt to seize the young male of the human species between the ages of sixteen and twenty-four. Its chief symptoms are, a wild desire to get back to what is natural, to find out the cause of everything, to reduce everything to first principles, to seize on generalities. A tendency to find no religion lofty enough, no political system perfect enough. Exalted but vague ambitions and ideals, great earnestness, restless but purposeless energy; and lastly, owing to the soul being literally born a second time, a babyish power of realising the infinite mystery and wonder of the most commonplace things, which makes the cool matter-of-course view of the rest of the world in general infinitely exasperating.

'A young man in this phase (take myself as an instance) always puts me in mind of a child seeing the moon for the first time, realising its awful wonder, and being intensely hurt and vexed with the dulness of grown-up people who are not in the least struck with the solemn unexplainable mystery of the spectacle.'

'Do you believe that most people go through this phase of second childhood on entering life?'

'A great many more than we suppose, to a greater or less extent. I never,' said he, smiling, 'see a remarkably fat, respectable, comfortable-looking old gentleman, who talks nothing but farming, three per cents, or ultra-Conservative politics, without thinking to myself, "My good old friend, there was a time when you were a sentimental republican at heart, and wrote poetry in secret."'

'What is the next phase to be?' asked I, laughing.

'God only knows,' replied he. 'Some subside in a very short time into mere jolly worldly take-it-easy cynicism; some rush into frantic religion; some remain on the same stilts all their life, and run their course in this world with an extra portion both of bitterness and pleasure; while others, though retaining their lofty ideals to the end, are strong enough to take the world as it is, and to turn their energy to whatever fraction of the great work may lie in their path, and lie down at last in peace, having contributed their mite to the happiness of their fellow-men.'

'Well,' said I, 'it seems that after enjoying two or three years of this mental stomach-ache, people become pretty much what they were before. What's the good of it?'

'People are *not* quite the same as they were before—after it; their few years of *Sturm und Drang* are the heating in the furnace which qualifies the metal; their effect, however invisible, is never quite lost. After the sharp miseries of conception the twice-born young soul rushes, with a titanic strength and energy unknown before, to the groove best suited for it. And the marks of this fiery second birth remain for ever. Ay! take a deep dive in your unconventional way into the depths of some character apparently bound entirely by conventional laws and inbred prejudices, and then you will startle into life a keen recollection of the days of wild beautiful ideas, and the terrible ordeal of doubts. That mind can never quite narrow itself again to the limits of mere *ignorant* prejudice. Even its fierce fanaticism has something distinctive about it. It is the bigotry of earnestness, not of mere dull conceited ignorance. You ask me what is the purpose of this ordeal. No man can tell God's reasons, but it seems to me as if, in order to prevent us becoming mere bundles of conventional instincts and inherited prejudices, He had ordained that a large proportion of us, on entering manhood, should have suddenly and rudely the whole of our past education and its influences torn from our souls for a space, forcing us back to refreshing nature and naked first principles on all subjects.'

'That's rather fanciful,' said I.

'It don't seem so to me,' replied he, 'because I think it is the key to the vastly superior progress of some nations over others. Chinamen—most Orientals—even Roman Catholic Europeans, drop behind in the race, simply because they have lost the knack of, or discountenance, this wild fermentation of mind at the beginning of manhood. There could be *no improvement* if all were orthodox, as it is called, on every subject. Wherefore let not the world be too hard on us mad young Berserkirs; one in a hundred of us does good to his kind.'

'And you call yourself a Conservative, you twisting young eel!' cried I. 'What rejoicing among the angels of my party there would be if they could have heard that last declaration of your opinion!'

'You old silly,' answered he, impudently, 'what I said don't compromise my British Conservatism in the least. I am a Conservative, and a staunch one, simply because, after going through a good many countries, this blessed New Zealand included, I have come to the human and fallible conclusion that the British constitution is, or was, the best in the world. I am a staunch Conservative, but of course no opponent to what I believe to be progress. I simply say, what you Liberals call progress, *i.e.* an advance towards democracy, I believe to be a step in the wrong direction in the nineteenth century, whatever it may be in the twenty-fifth.'

Political conversations are, holds my young friend, newspaper articles without their good English, so we become silent by mutual consent, and gaze dreamily at the gorgeous sunset. The sea had turned to a pale dull oily gray, the torn fragments of summer cloud were changing their gorgeous golden and scarlet hues for modest pink and white, and of the fierce radiance that so lately inflamed the sky nothing remained but a deep fiery glow behind the blackening hills, marking the wake of the day.

My young friend, with his face between his hands, was gazing northward across the sleeping ocean as if his eyes could almost reach the lovely islands of the tropics, murmuring to himself a wild old South Sea poem:

' Lay me down on the deck, my lad, with my face towards the bow.
 They say there is land in sight; but my eyes are failing now.
 Young though I be, my course is run. It seems so hard to die,
 With the fresh sea sparkling round me, and the land I love so nigh.
 You say the land's rising quick, Bill, but I know that I shall not last;
 I'm going soon, for already the pain of this cursed wound is past.

It was not the whale, poor betch, she never 'ud do one
    harm,
But ye see my foot slipped, and that thundering lubber
    Jem, he jogged my arm.
I'd like to see Tahiti, with its flowers and fruit, once more,
With its wild blue mountains rising up from the palm-trees
    on the shore,
The trees 'neath which I've lain and spent so many happy
    hours,
While the wild girls lolled around and rigged my head
    with their bright wild flowers ;
Sleeping, and sucking cocoa-nuts, and kissing, the livelong
    day.
I knows they weren't always faithful, Bill, but they never
    axed for pay.
You mind a lass called Nita, the last time as we was there,
Tall and strong, with glistening eyes, and coal-black
    rippling hair?
I loved her true, and when I left I promised to come
    again,
And now I shall never see her more. It'll give the poor
    lass pain.
I'd like to see—but what matter now? I know that I'm
    going fast.
I'll be signing my mark in another ship's books before
    this watch is past ;
To-morrow, Bill, you'll launch me away to my home in
    the deep blue sea.
I'll have a glorious grave, indeed, the whole of the ocean
    free !
I'll deck myself out with the small coral-fish, those ones
    with a brilliant blue,
And them, you know, like butterflies, all of a golden
    hue ;
And I'll choose a patch of silvery sand in the coral to lay
    my head,
There isn't a king in the wide, wide world, will have such
    a lovely bed.

.   .   .   .   .

You say that the land is nigh, but my eyes are failing now,
Lay me down on the deck, my lad, with my face towards the bow.'

'If that ballad,' say I, 'wasn't coarse, and so very rough in expression, it would be rather fine.'

'And yet,' replied he, 'if you eliminated its coarseness and polished its expression you would take away its reality, and consequently its pathos. It is that wild, coarse, misty ignorance of the poor dying whaler, contrasting, yet blending, with his innate, strange, poetic feeling, that gives it at once its sadness and its truth.'

'You are very tiresome about poetry,' cried I. 'You are ridiculously sentimental about any doggerel ballad; but when I give you some lofty spiritual poetry to read, such as Newman's "Dream of Gerontius," or Myers's "St. Paul," you fly into a tumult of rage and scorn, rave of their base prurient materialism and their windy nonsense in one breath, and parody them with a merciless vandalism of which you ought to be ashamed.'

'Because they try to do something above their powers. They try to soar above humanity, and consequently sink below it. To get beyond (as they fancy) their earthiness they work themselves into a religious ecstasy, which requires to be fed by a tangible, materialistic, and often prurient idea of spiritual things; mix this with a proper leaven of windy wordy nonsense, and you have a religious poem of the kind you have mentioned. So, as no one can write superhuman poetry to please me, I content myself with poems breathing the beauties of humanity, of which we all know something, taking perhaps for my type of perfection Hood's "Bridge of Sighs."'

'But surely,' say I, 'for all your sneering, this kind of ecstatic religious fervour does us good, by raising our thoughts from the sordid earth to a sense of the reality of higher things?'

'Sordid earth, indeed!' retorts he, scornfully. 'You people who use that argument seem to be possessed by an idea that God placed you in the world just to prove that you were a great deal too good for it. Leave such notions of the vileness of God's work to shallow-pated young priests and vain ecstatic young ladies. Why try to raise ourselves above the earth (if it be possible) while there is higher divinity, vaster beauty, in the everyday life around us than our little souls can take in in a lifetime, in spite of its tangibility?'

'And so, most inconsistent of young persons, you who rave against the deification of man in all existing religions are as great a humanity worshipper as any!' cried I, triumphantly.

'With a slight difference,' answered he, drily. 'I love and try to learn from my brother, whom I do know, but don't for a moment assume that he is a likeness of God, whom I don't know.'

'I think,' said I, branching off, 'that you carry your humanity worship almost too far. You love even its imperfections. None of your beloved characters in poetry and prose are by any means faultless. A perfect saint you don't love half as much as a good-hearted sinner, as long as he has no meanness about him. You take after your great idol, the cynical Thackeray, who would go a mile out of his way to find a hole in the coat of any man with an appearance of respectability, and handled a good-for-nothing Bohemian with the loving tenderness of a mother with her first baby.'

'A soulless godless world calls Thackeray a bitter cynic, chiefly because they do not understand him, partly because he is an undying reproach to their hypocritical shams and heathen selfishness. They would have said the same of One whom Thackeray worshipped, had they lived in those days. He was no mere cold-blooded disbeliever in the constancy and honour and generosity of mankind because he did not possess them himself; his bitterness sprang from an earnest love of the virtues he daily saw counterfeited and neglected. A cynical heartless remark, that in many circles, both high and low, would pass without notice or comment, struck bitter anger and sorrow into his more loving sensitive soul. Still worse, when time after time he, an earnest lover and seeker of what is good and noble, rushed eagerly at the appearance of it, and found he had grasped a sham. And thus he, not unlike the great Master that he served, learnt to pour out all his warm love and forgiveness to the simple warm-hearted sinner, and to hold the more sinless, but hypocritical and self-complacent Pharisee, in loathing and disgust.

'And they say he was a disbeliever in human goodness!—he who revelled in the simple, manly, boyish purity of a character like Clive Newcome's until we are infected with his enthusiasm, hardly knowing why; he who loved and believed in goodness so much that he could dwell fondly over the rather insipid virtues of Amelia! Who but a man with an *intense* love and faith in human goodness and nobility could have drawn Warrington? A sketch dim, misty, imperfect, yet, owing to the warm intensity of its creator's feeling, a living picture, before which we can remain for ever with the tears in our eyes and a love in our hearts which seem almost absurdly wasted upon a mere phantasm of a writer's brain.

'And how beautiful, how almost piteous, is his triumphant exultation when, having drawn the faults, and even meannesses, of some lifelike human character, as scrupulously and sternly as though he were forced to it by some spell, he seizes on some little trait of warm, noble, human feeling! I tell you that man was no mere sour caviller, but more like one who, having his perceptions of good and evil sharpened by some purer spiritual atmosphere, was grieved and angered by our meanness, yet loved and worshipped all that was noble in our nature from the bottom of his great sore heart.'

'You are an idolater,' cried I, 'and, moreover,

a polytheist; for you nearly blew me into space yesterday for saying I didn't care for Dickens. How many more demigods am I to put into my calendar?'

'Bulwer Lytton and Charles Kingsley will do for the present,' answered he, laughing; 'but you mustn't suppose that because I pitched into your feminine lack of appreciation of humour yesterday you are to put that delightful literary acrobat, Dickens, on to the same pedestal with my sublime Thackeray. I have studied Dickens unceasingly since I was ten years old, and yet the only *personal* feeling I have got towards the author is gratitude for having given so many hours of great pleasure and amusement. I never learnt anything from him; my inner self was never touched and changed by any of his words. To put it shortly, I read Dickens for his books and Thackeray for himself.

'In one sense Dickens's writing is a most charming literary *tour de force*. When his delightfully grotesque creations are sent for a time into the background, and the author himself comes forward and tries to be didactic or sentimental, I skip; for when he is didactic he is provokingly bumptious; when he uses sentiment he elaborates it artificially till I can't swallow it. His Nells and Smikes won't draw water into my eyes after the first reading.

'With Thackeray it is different. Call it a literary fault, if you will; he himself is the most interesting character in all his books. In every work he seems to say, " Here am I, with a living world round me. I will paint a small fragment of it exactly as I see it. I claim for my pictures no merit of invention, only the merit of being true to life. Reader, let us go hand in hand and talk and think over their faults and virtues together."

'And it is his intuitive knowledge of when to let a picture speak for itself that gives him such a power of pathos. It is its terrible simplicity of narration, its hideous commonplaceness (I don't know if you understand what I mean), that makes the description of that poor blackguard Rawdon Crawley's discovery of his wife's deceit so undyingly touching. The story of the catastrophe is told without a comment. And then, when poor Rawdon, crushed, wild, and broken-hearted, goes to his prim, shallow, respectable brother, to tell him, the latter naturally begins the conversation with the presupposed idea that Rawdon has come to borrow money of him. There is something awfully cruel in this simple truth. The contrast between the utter despair of Rawdon's mind and the petty irritation of that of his obtuse brother is rendered more ghastly by its natural commonplaceness. And the next touch, when even the shallow despicable Pitt is really moved with awe and pity at the great grief he finds himself in the presence of, derives its beauty from its truth to nature. And then, poor Rawdon goes to Macmurdo to ask him to act as his second, and the good-natured, Epicurean, jolly old soldier sympathises with him as far as a man of his kind, who has led his kind of life, can—and that is not far. Again a contrast—horribly cruel, horribly simple and natural. You feel that poor Rawdon's ignorant untrained soul is alone for the first time with a great agonising grief, and the whole picture is so horribly lifelike that you find yourself saying, "Poor fellow! poor fellow!" with a choke in your voice, ay, though you read it fifty times.'

'And yet,' said I, 'you profess to disbelieve in a devil. You! you! with your horrible power of realising the misery of things, from the squashing of a wasp to the breaking of a heart? Why, your mind has greater necessity for a devil than any I know.'

'So a devil is necessary to me, is it?' answered he, a little grimly. 'Well, well, you are touching a great truth. "The Devil," like many another dogma, holds his place in men's minds because he fills a gap they dislike. I tell you there is a conviction growing daily in my mind that all religious theories and dogmas spring from or are connected with *one* want. Theories in all creeds of falls of man, redemptions, future rewards and punishments, extinction, devils, sins, and so on, *ad libitum*, spring from the same source. If I were asked to define what is a religion as shortly as possible, I should say, "An attempt to account for the origin, purpose, and nature, of what we men call *pain* as comfortably to ourselves as possible." What matter if these explanatory dogmas that we console ourselves with lead to perpetual contradictions, blasphemies, and absurdities. Better that, says the conceit of human nature, than to own such mysteries beyond our reach. Oh, that insufferable, ignorant self-importance of man! Making all his religious theories contain one word for God and two for himself!

'Man! man! you blind mole! study nature; learn all you can of the universe around you; and if you do this, not merely as a schoolboy learns Latin lines by heart, but make your mind deduce from what you see, you will learn some lessons. You will find out the extremely narrow limits of human knowledge—man's insignificance in the universe; you will find that every commonplace thing, traced back, is an utterly insoluble mystery. And having once realised these bitter things, you will get a feeling of God's utterly unreachable, ungraspable magnitude that you never felt before. And from this last conviction comes peace of mind at last. From the bitter lesson of your own small worth and importance, and that of His inconceivable, unintelligible power, you will get a " faith," a childish, fatalistic trust, that will make your previous miseries of doubt, and longings for revelation concerning your existence and destiny, seem like a laughable dream. You will cry, as I do now, " Fool that I am, that know the narrow limits of my mind, that can realise that *every* simple thing around me is a mystery beyond my reach; that can feel from these things how inconceivable He is, and yet can flinch from blindly trusting that little atom, myself, and all my destiny, to Him! Shall I, in my foolish conceit and ignorance, cry for a knowledge that He has seen fit to deny to my race, and keep waiting for a revelation till I make an artificial one to comfort myself with?" Well, well! this religion won't come in our time, as I said to you the other day; so let us go back to the Devil, and the reasons why I can't believe in him. I believe that he was born (like many another article of faith) out of that absurd presumption that our notions of right and wrong are divine, not merely in the sense of being intended by God for us, but in the sense of being *applicable to God Himself and His actions.* In this wise. Man said, "There is a God," and the highest thing he could conceive being (as it is to this day), a perfect man, he created Him in the spiritual image of man, with a man's ideas of good and evil. But here a difficulty presented itself. If God was a being with our notions of justice and mercy, and also all-powerful over the universe, how came what man calls pain and sin? A theory of a Devil, that is to say, an antagonistic power of evil, apparently solved the difficulty. I say apparently, because really it leaves the problem nearly where it was; for it is just as monstrous to believe that a Supreme Being with our notions of justice and mercy, and having almighty power, would allow an evil spirit to gratify his cruelty on us, as to believe that He does it Himself. The disciples of Zoroaster avoided this difficulty by making the good spirit and the evil one of equal power. But such a theory, besides being contrary to the teachings of the simplest natural science (don't sneer), is utterly repugnant to our feelings —more terrible than even the coldest, blankest rationalism.'

'What you call science is liable to err,' said I.

'So it seems is religion,' replied he, drily ; 'for I never met a religious man of *any* creed, who did not think that all religions but one were more or less false. When will religious people learn this evident but humiliating truth :

"'If it were not for the merest accident of birth,
You might have been high priest to Mumbo Jumbo?"'

But there is this to be said, that, if they did realise fully this truth, it would take half the power for good out of their religion. Depend upon it, that a little bigotry, a little narrow-mindedness, is a good and useful thing. *If men were not thoroughly convinced of the absolute truth of the creed they hold, what power (except in a few exceptional cases) would it have to direct their actions?* And so, though I don't believe in the Devil, because I think I see his human origin ; because his existence seems to be a blasphemy against God, because all nature (of which man is part), denies a divided power, I see that, like many another human dogma, he is useful in the great work of improvement, and could not be dispensed with, at present, without harm.'

'I don't yet quite understand your standpoint on these subjects,' said I; 'you are continually on both sides of the hedge. You take some so-called revealed fact out of a religion, pull it to pieces, show its human origin, the contradictions, and blasphemies it leads to, give a lot of reasons which prevent you from believing in it, and then coolly turn round and say it is good for men to believe in, etc.'

'What,' cried he, 'would you have me put myself on the level of the lowest form of missionary, and say, for instance, "I do not believe in the tenets of Hinduism?—I feel sure they are not God's truth, therefore Hinduism cannot have benefited mankind, and most likely has done it harm?" Away with such blasphemy—for blasphemy it is. Are we to deny that the world and all it contains have a Divine origin? Are we to say that the many religions of the earth are here in defiance of His will? I, the sceptic, at least, believe so firmly in God's great all-pervading power as to feel convinced that all around me is made by Him with a purpose, whether I know it or not; have faith enough in Him to feel convinced that these religions, whose tenets I cannot believe in, are part of His great developing plan, the end of which I cannot even guess at. And holding this trusting fatalistic faith in Him, how can I dare to look at any portion of His work, and in my insignificant human knowlege say, "I know better, this ought not to be?"

> '"Nay, friend, think not that I am one of those
> Who calmly claim omniscience, and suppose
> That God Almighty scarcely knows the worth
> Of this or that existing on the earth,
> And cry, False creeds I cannot bear to see,
> Because I'm sure that God agrees with me."'

'Well, that's all very well,' said I, 'but it seems to me that this extreme humility and perfect trust that you not unnaturally triumph in must lead to sheer fatalism, and from that to simple indifference. If the mass of mankind believed, as you do, that the whole world, with its good and evil contents, was a great plan, in which they were merely automata, they would simply put their hands in their pockets and loaf away their lives without a purpose, and all improvement, humanly speaking, would come to an end.'

'Well,' answered he, coolly, 'haven't I told you so often before?—(not that fatalism *always* produces indifference, but it, at any rate, seems to be the natural consequence of it). But now you will see why I am always on both sides of the hedge, as you call it. This conviction of the uselessness of my negative creed to mankind forces me to see the good of religions, and to understand, *from the deficiencies* of my own scheme, how and why they produce virtue. And then, you see, my firm conviction that we are all part of God's plan of improvement, makes me believe that the narrow-minded man, who deems that his opinions alone are God's truth, is doing His work, shows me how his very narrowness and fanaticism are of good use, while none the less are men of the school to which I belong working in the same scheme by opposing his want of liberality. I might go on for ever on this theme. As in nature, so in men, opposing forces producing results. I cannot imagine a greater evil for mankind than the sudden loss of the superstitions and fallacies that they now believe in, excepting the utter destruction of that puny whisper in favour of greater liberality that is now always affecting their hearts, if not their heads.

'Yes, I am continually on both sides of the hedge. Confirmed sceptic though I be, the invariable conclusion that all my speculations lead to is the superior power for good of almost any religion (that is to say, any scheme that professes to throw light on mysteries beyond the reach of human investigation) over the noblest, purest form of what is called scepticism. The very humility, the want of assumption of knowledge of the latter, makes it unattractive to men and powerless to direct their actions; the very perfection of its trust in God tends to fatalism and indifference.

'Is it not strange how extremes meet? The stronghold of a pious Romanist is his blind faith, that of the sceptic his complete trust in God. The slur so often cast against the former is his toleration of pious frauds; and here am I, the sceptic, with all my contempt for dishonesty of thought, forced into a respect for their utility, both by my conscience and senses. Ay! I respect pious frauds. Though the presumption, and superstition, and uncharitable exclusiveness of every religion move me with pity, with horror, with contempt, I cannot shut my eyes to the fact that the good that they do far outweighs the evil —far outweighs the good that could be done by a negative humble creed like mine. And in them I see the finger of God leading mankind on the march towards greater purity and virtue in the manner best suited to them. Who am I that I should not bow my head and say, It is good?'

'Then why,' asked I, rather stupidly, 'if you feel the worthlessness of your belief as compared to religion, don't you leave it?'

'Why?' cried he, opening his eyes and half laughing. 'Why, how can I leave my creed unless it leaves me? Belief ought to be a matter of conscience, not compulsion. Ah, well! You orthodox people never can appreciate our only virtue—a sacred fearless unbribable honesty of thought. Supposing I (if it were possible to me, which I don't believe) were to force or persuade myself to believe anything because I knew it would be good and pleasant for me to believe it, my conscience would tell me that I was committing a great crime—a moral suicide. But come; it is as dark as pitch, and if we don't want to be drowned or break our necks we had better be getting homewards.'

And so we scrambled home in silence through the murmuring forest, occasionally lighted by weird moon flashes through the shivering trees,—for the land breeze had sprung up,—pondering each over our own thoughts. And as I thought over all he had said, I could not help being struck by the glorious loftiness of the position from which he judged the world, by his power in seeing good in what he hated, but still more by the uselessness of this position—useless except in the negative way of mitigating bigotry and partisanship on all sides. Would he, too, some day, buckle on the armour of life and come down to fight in God's cause on one side or another?

Time will show.

CHAPTER III

I WAS standing in front of our little cottage in a state of perplexity. Twenty yards before me, caulking the bottom of his beloved sailing-boat, knelt my young philosophical friend, bare-throated, bare-armed, bare-footed, and coatless, as male creatures of all classes generally are in the summer in this barbarous, out-of-the-way little corner of the world.

'Charlie,' cry I, in a most humble, entreating voice, 'are you very busy?'

'Never am—never was—never shall be, in this world, I think,' was his laconic answer.

'Dan Stringer's wife's got a baby,' continue I, in the same tone.

'I don't quite see,' replied he, with mock gravity, 'what that has to do with my being busy; nor why you should announce this extraordinary fact, as if you thought it a national calamity.'

'Don't be silly,' said I; 'I mean that of course I must take her some things, and find what she wants, and so on. And it's such an awful walk over the hills, and through the forest, round to Dan's hut, especially if one has a horrid great bundle to carry.'

'Hens,' said he, provokingly seating himself on the bottom of his boat, and pointing at me solemnly with a roll of tow, 'are more sensible than women on such occasions. When a hen lays an egg she sits on that egg, and does her duty by that egg, as a matter of course, unassisted by any of her female friends; but when a——'

'Oh, if you won't, I suppose I must manage as best I can,' interrupted I, half angrily.

'Won't what?' replied he, trying to look astonished. 'I'm not aware that you've asked me to do anything yet. Now, to save time, allow me to say what you want to express. "Dear Charlie, will you get out your skiff, and row me and my bundle of unnecessaries up to the creek at the head of the harbour as quick as you can (the distance is only five miles, and the thermometer only a hundred and ten in the shade), and then carry the bundle for me up to the cottage; and then, after I have satisfied my feminine love of cackling and fussing about, during which time you can amuse yourself by looking after the boat, row me back again by moonlight?" Cut along, and get the bundle—old gowns, mysterious linen, flannel, jelly, chickens, and the rest of it; and I'll have the boat out by the time you're ready.'

'Oh, thank you so much,' cried I, scuttling off; and behold me presently, my bundle having been already safely deposited in the boat, balancing myself on the top of a slippery rock, trying to get in. The first thing I did was nearly to topple forward into the sea; the next thing, naturally, was to topple backwards on to an oyster bed—a most unpleasant thing to tumble on. Having regained the treacherous rock, I did manage, somehow, to find myself in the boat on top of my bundle; my young friend only commenting on my adventures with, 'If you don't sit steady, we shall be spilt into the drink! Trim dish!'

In a minute, propelled by long, powerful strokes, we had rounded the rocky point which formed the corner of the little bay in which our house stood, and were in the long, narrow, main harbour, heading straight for our destination.

'*House*, indeed!' thought I, laughing to myself as I remembered the old country. 'If some agent on a large English property saw that wooden dwelling, with only four rooms and a shed at the back, and no upstairs in it, and was told that it was a *house*, in which lived and were happy an ex-colonel of the line, his wife, and six children, he would have a fit.'

Away we went swiftly through the clear, calm water, the creaking of the straining rowlocks, and the swish and bubble of the water echoing amongst the steep, wooded cliffs on each side of us. There is nothing to me so pleasant as being rowed by an expert sculler in smooth water. The swish of the sculls, and the measured cadence with which they strike the water—the lifting, bubbling rush at the commencement of the stroke, and the long, steady shoot that follows—give a feeling, somehow, of strength and courage that makes rowing, above all things, the 'poetry of motion.'

No one who has not seen one of these inland harbours has a notion of their extraordinary romantic beauty. Imagine a long, narrow arm of the sea winding for four or five miles through sunlit, cloud-shadowed, forest-clad hills. On each side of you, as you pass each bold, rocky bluff, with weird-looking crags starting out of its very face, you open out some snug, fairylike little bay, with, most likely, a little creek running into its head, with, perhaps, a little cottage on the bank— a tiny finger-mark of man on the glorious expanse of untamed nature. Far behind the cottage will run up into the hills a steep-sided, wooded gully, such as New Zealand alone can show, with all its glories of *kauri* pine and tree-fern ; and as you gaze up the chasm, and away beyond it, you see

> 'Far out, kindled by each other,
> Shining hills on hills arise ;
> Close as brother leans to brother,
> When they press beneath the eyes
> Of some father praying blessings from the gifts of Paradise.'

Oh, the charm of these little water-nooks! To slip on a hot, still summer's day into their quiet shade, to let your boat glide under the overhanging branches of some majestic *pohutikawa*, and there read, or more likely dream away, half the day. To lie there, thinking new thoughts and old, or painting in your mind visions of glorious scenes and noble deeds, till you begin to feel tearfully in love with all humanity; while the mullet, unconscious of your presence, plays joyfully upon the surface of the still water, while the little bell-bird sends forth his round, clear notes from the branches above your head; and the sarcastic *tui*, 'the *nil admirari* man' amongst birds, parodies him with the most shameless Vandalism.

'Disgraceful idleness'—'A most mischievous and dangerous habit'—say some of my friends—all the more energetically, perhaps, because they can't understand the pleasure that is to be derived from it. Well, well! Though I honour the spirit that wrote

> 'Be good, sweet maid, and let who will be clever;
>   Do noble things, not dream them all day long;
> Making past, present, and the vast forever
>   One grand sweet song—'

I think that there are some spirits that would be utterly crushed and destroyed by the accumulated petty miseries of this life, if not occasionally refreshed by glimpses of some kind of heaven through the medium of dreamland. To some it would be simply spirit-death never to be allowed to dream of things beyond the petty commonplaces of life. Ay! and I am by no means sure that I envy those even-minded people who, in scenes like these, never feel the spell take possession of them, glorious in its beauty and its pleasure, almost terrible in its limitless immensity. For at these moments we are ever creeping to the very brink of the precipice, and vainly trying to peer into that vast, bottomless chasm—'the Unknowable.' Is there nothing glorious in the hours when our existing selves and our commonplace life become shadowy, and the mysteries of our being and our future real living facts? In those moments, when

> 'Each thought, as it forms and rises,
>   Is full of a solemn awe.
> Wildly it breaks and scatters
>   The germs of a thousand more.
> Onward and ever onward
>   The old thoughts lead to new,
> Waking and fading together,
>   The false lights and the true.
>
> 'Truths unrevealed show dimly
>   And pass with a fitful gleam,
> The marks of the soul's great battles
>   Flit past like a misty dream,
> Winding and changing quickly,
>   Clashing at times in strife,
> Yet their bitterness all softened
>   By the spell of their Spirit-life.'

. . . . .

'What a beautiful idea,' remarked my young friend, slackening his stroke in order to talk, and gazing dreamily at a gorgeous bit of *kauri* forest at the top of the ridge, 'the Maories have in their tradition of creation, of the Earth and the Sky in the first period of Great Darkness, when they were lying one on top of the other, being forced apart by the forest trees, until "in these latter days Heaven remains far removed from his wife the Earth; but the love of the wife is wafted up in sighs towards her husband. These are the mists which fly upwards from the mountain tops, and the tears of Heaven fall downward on his wife. Behold the dewdrops!"'[1]

'I never could make head or tail of Maori mythology,' said I. 'In most of their traditions one seems forced to own that either their meaning is so terribly deep that one can't reach it, or else that they are simply silly stories.'

'There are many things that make it difficult,' replied he. 'In the first place, I believe it is almost impossible to translate Maori meaning into English meaning (if you understand me). Again,

[1] This quotation is taken from an unpublished paper called *The Maori Tradition of Creation*, written by the old Pakeha Maori, the talented author of *Old New Zealand*, etc. It is a literal translation of the oral traditions of the *tohungas* (priests), communicated to him after goodness knows how many solemn vows, mystic initiations, and bargains with the Devil. He gave it to me with a solemn injunction to hold my tongue about it as long as I was in the country. Even now I dare not publish it, strongly tempted as I am to do so, by the romantic beauty of its allegories and their deep meaning, lest in a few months the neighbourhood of New Burlington Street should be startled by a select band of strapping young fellows calling at No. 8 to inquire the names, weights, and addresses of the editor and all the contributors. So I must content myself with the very baldest outline of the sacred mysteries.

the traditions being merely orally transmitted from one priest to another, and the said priests having gradually lost sight of the meaning of many of the allegories, a stray word or expression has occasionally unconsciously been altered, until it becomes almost impossible to read the spirit of the original version. Again, later traditions have crept in, mixing themselves with the older ones, till the mass gets as hopelessly inconsistent as the book of Gen——'

'Stop!' cried I. 'If once you begin on that subject you will be a monomaniac for a week. Let's hear what you have got to say about the Maori one.'

'Very well,' replied he, smiling. 'Listen. The Maori tradition of creation, like the Jewish one (I groaned, but he took no notice), wisely does not profess to begin at the beginning of the world; in fact, neither of them are really an account of creation, but rather of development. Both the Jewish and the Maori traditions begin by stating the previous existence of the world, and strangely enough, neither attempt to account for its existence. The Jew says that at the time his history commences it was in a state of chaos, which always seems to me a disrespectful way of thinking about God's works; the Maori says it was in a state of uninhabitable darkness, or rather, in his mythical, poetical way, that the Heavens lay upon the bosom of the Earth, and this was the time of the Great Night. Then at last life[1] commenced, and the

[1] Not meaning human, nor even animal life, perhaps.

five children of the sun and earth resolved to separate them, all but the wind spirit, who was grieved by their cruelty. All tried, but only the forest god succeeded. "Thus, by the destruction of their parents, they sought to make life increase and flourish; and in commemoration of these things are the traditionary sayings, The night! the night! The day! the day! The searching, the struggling for the light! the light!"[1] (Do you not think we may look on this as a most beautiful allegory of the struggles of nature towards organisation?)

'But the storm spirit followed his father, Heaven, and resolved to make war on his brethren because they had separated his parents, and he attacked them with his children, the winds and the great rains. Tane Makuta, the forest god, went down like a reed before him. He would also have destroyed Ronga Matane and Kamia, the gods of tame and wild plants, but the Earth hid them in her bosom. Then his wrath was turned against Tangaroa, the ocean god, and he drove him away from the cliffs that he washed against. But the family of Tangaroa now divided: the swimming-fish taking to the sea, and Consternation, the great reptile, to the land. (The geological meaning of this allegory is too simple, I think, to need explanation.)

'Then the victorious storm god attacked the youngest of all his brothers, the mysterious Tu.

[1] *The Maori Tradition of Creation.*

(How shall I call him? Odin Allfather; the war god, the god of destruction; *above all, " the spirit of man."*) But the warrior Tu stood upright and defied him. Then Tu resolved to make war against his brethren because they had not assisted him resolutely against the storm, and he set traps for the children of the forest gods (birds), and soon they were hanging in the trees. " He sought the children of Tangaroa, and found them swimming in the sea. He cuts the flax, he knots the net, he draws it in the water. Ha! the sons of Tangaroa are dying on the shore. And now he seeks his brethren, Ronga and Kamia, whom the Earth had concealed from the storm; but their hair appearing above the ground betrayed them. Now with the stone wedge he bursts the hardwood tree, and forms the pointed *ko*, the Maori spade. Now he weaves baskets, now he digs the earth. Ronga and Kamia lie drying in the sun. . . . Then Tu sought prayers and incantations, by which to depress his brethren and reduce them to the condition of common food for himself. He had also incantations for the winds, to cause a calm; prayers for children, wealth, abundant crops, fair weather, and also for the souls of men. . . . During the war with the storm the greater part of the earth was overwhelmed by the waters. . . . The light now continued to increase, and as the light increased, so the life that had been hidden between heaven and earth increased; also Tu and his *elder* brethren, who had existed during the first great darkness, during the seeking and struggling, when old Earthquake reigned." And so generation was added to generation down to the time of Mani-Potiki, who brought death into the world.

'Now this allegory seems simply to be a wild poetical account of the gradual fermentation of life in nature; then the destruction of the rank uninhabitable forests by floods and storms; also the first development of reptiles from fish; and lastly, the *gradual* victory of man over surrounding nature. If you don't want to go mad, examine into these traditions no further; for just as you think gleefully that you are beginning to understand what the scheme was, you will be met by some startling piece of extraneous information that utterly upsets and contradicts everything that has gone before. When you have despairingly choked and shut your eyes to this difficulty, and are imagining yourself, as you read on through the tradition, having a capital bit of swamp-shooting amongst the lively pterodactyls, you come across some such anachronism as

'" Fairshon had a son
Who married Noah's daughter,
And nearly spoiled ta Flood
By drinking up ta water."

If this don't make you give it up in despair, the meaning of some name—Tu, for instance—will nearly finish you. At one moment you find it meaning, apparently, life; at the next, intelligence;

at the next, simply man; at the next, the god of war, etc. This, combined with countless allegories, purposely mystified at first, accidentally mystified afterwards, until the original meaning has been lost, worse still, allegories altered to apply to later events—in short, an accumulated muddle of dates, words, and ideas—will bring you to the conclusion that it is better to study Maori theology for the sake of its occasional poetical glimpses of grand truths than to try and reduce it to a consistent scheme. One can only think with a sigh, what a pity it is that such a many-meaninged no-meaninged muddle should be wasted on the nineteenth century, instead of being in vogue in the Middle Ages, when it might have afforded endless work and interest to countless theologians, besides supplying continual amusing spectacles, in the shape of *autos-da-fé*, to their lighter-hearted fellows.

'But there are some peculiarities of the Maori religion which are well worth noting, either caused by or causing some of the strangest traits of the Maori character. You remember my saying the other day that all religions were attempts to explain the origin, purpose, etc., of pain as comfortably to ourselves as possible. I confess the Maori almost upsets my theory. With the exception of a careless mention of Maui, the Maori Hercules, having brought human death into the world by disobeying a demi-god, he treats this subject with stoical indifference or Odin-like triumph. When the children of heaven and earth are plotting how to separate their parents, what cries the man spirit, Tu?—" Let us destroy them both!" The antagonism and destruction that he describes as producing development he takes with a kind of triumphant stoicism, as a matter of course ; he does not even distress himself enough about the origin and purpose of pain to invent a theory of a devil. He goes no further than to think that when a man is sick he is possessed by an *atua*, or ghoul. He has no idea of a good, *merciful* spirit, above him, to supplicate in his hour of sorrow, no higher conception of prayer than *charming* a spirit by performing certain incantations correctly. The first converts to Christianity retained this feeling (if not, indeed, the later ones), and before attacking their neighbours would repeat a Christian hymn word for word, attributing their defeat, if they were thrashed, to some one having left out a syllable accidentally. In short, their religion was extraordinarily godless, devilless, compassionless, stoical, and defiant.

'The missionaries, dear, simple souls, were delighted to find that the old Maori creed was so extraordinarily like the old Jewish one ; never seeing that it was those very points, held in common by both, that made the conversion of the Jews impossible.'

' How can you call the religion of the Old Testament godless?' asked I, astonished.

' I used a vague word for want of a better,' replied he. ' I meant by "godless," a low, narrow, practical view of a Deity. What Jehovah was to the Jews in the days of Moses and Joshua, Tu was to the Maories. Jehovah was the God who confined his favour to the Jewish tribe, Tu to the Maori one. All through the Old Testament seems to run the same pæan: "Is not our God stronger than those of other nations?" Like Tu, he was a God of death and vengeance, with still stronger personal animosities. Both seemed to have valued their gods simply for their superior power. Elijah converted the Israelites who had taken to Baal-worship by demonstrating the superior power of Jehovah. The same feeling made the Maories rush eagerly at Christianity on its first introduction, saying that ships, fire-arms, etc., proved the superior power of the Christian God to their own. (When they found their mistake they dropped it as quickly as they had taken it up.)

'Their ways of *tapu*ing themselves before going to battle are literally identical, and both Jew and Maori priest accounted for defeat in exactly the same manner, *i.e.* the god being displeased because some one had broken the *tapu*. The story of Achan before Ai is Maori to the very letter. In short, if any one asked me for information concerning the old Maori religion, I should say, "Read your Old Testament literally, without looking out for types and prophecies, and you will catch both its rites and its spirit nearly exactly." I have no doubt that Joshua and Te Waharoa, Gideon and Heke, spin each other many a grand old fighting yarn in the land of spirits; and that Samuel has found many a sympathetic friend on Agag questions among the stern old *tohungas* of the South Seas. So great was the similarity between the two religions that when the Old Testament was, by an unfortunate mistake, translated into Maori, it was greedily seized upon by the natives, to the utter ruin of the skin-deep Christianity that they professed.

'Like as they are in some ways to the old Jews, they differ on one or two points that make the chance of converting them to true Christianity still more hopeless; for they have a far less definite religious feeling, and a far more careless, stoical way of looking at both good and evil fortune. The glorious comforts of many of the Christian doctrines are looked on by the Maori with the greatest indifference.'

'So you don't think,' said I, 'that they will ever become *real* Christians.'

'There will be no time to make them so, I fancy, for in a hundred years or so they will have ceased to exist as a distinct race, and it is madness to suppose that they can be thoroughly altered in a generation or two. That is a fact that both many of the missionaries and many of those who abuse them often forget. They seem to think that two babies of different races born into the world are fitted with a couple of souls not necessarily very different in their tendencies until tampered with by people and circumstances.

It is a most fatal mistake. As the Maori baby is brown and the other one pink, white, or mottled, so their little souls have on them the impress of the instincts, laws, prejudices, and so on, of a thousand ancestors. And consequently, in many cases, although you take the little savage away from evil communications, teach him to cut his cannibalistic little teeth on civilised india-rubber, educate him with a view to the ministry, and dress him in the tight clothes and shining boots of the pale-face, it often happens that, on his arrival at the age of indiscretion, he bolts for the home of his fathers, and is next heard of eating the warm liver of some unfortunate colonist! *You have not got to convert merely a single soul, but a mixture of thousands.* Hallo! 'Ware mangroves!'

We had now reached the mangrove swamp that nearly always lies at the head of a New Zealand harbour, and were picking our way through it towards the mouth of the creek that emptied itself into their hideous forest. Oh, those mangroves! I never saw one that looked as if it possessed a decent conscience. Growing always in shallow stagnant water, filthy black mud, or rank grass, gnarled, twisted, stunted, and half bare of foliage, they seem like crowds of withered trodden-down old criminals, condemned to the punishment of everlasting life. I can't help it, if this seems fanciful; any one who has seen a mangrove swamp will know what I mean. A minute more brought us to the creek, and we glided onwards under the network of branches, till we were stopped by an enormous *kauri* that had fallen right across it at the foot of the gully. So we landed, and, having made the boat fast, commenced scrambling upwards through the bush along the steep side of the ravine, sending stones and earth rolling down into the little creek, to the evident amusement of a jocose parrot, who followed and watched our progress with the greatest interest and amusement.

At last, hot and breathless, we emerged into an open glade, and came in view of a rude, comfortable-looking cottage. Out rushed two tawny little scamps at the sight of my young friend, stiffening, however, into sulky rigidity as my petticoated figure emerged from the bush, followed immediately by the stately form of Dan himself. Dan is rather a typical man in bush life. Standing six feet three inches on his bare feet, shaped like a Hercules, and always in perfect training, he could cut more lengths of timber in a day, swear harder at bullocks, was a better hand amongst pigs and wild cattle, a better fisherman, a better oar, and a better boat-sailer than any man on the island, except perhaps my young friend, who rivalled him in the three latter capacities. Between the two there was a strong friendship, differences of rank not making much of a gulf in these places between Dives and Lazarus, for the bush has a strange power of 'bringing people together as wouldn't otherwise meet.' He had come out to New Zealand as a sailor-boy, had run his ship and joined a woodcutter's gang, and had finally located himself on our island, where he had taken to himself one of the daughters of the land for wife, who, after presenting him with half a dozen olive-skinned olive branches, had departed to the land of spirits. After a decent period of mourning, which I must say he bore most philosophically, he went up to Auckland, and to the great surprise of his friends returned in a week's time with a wife—a real white one—the interesting lady I had come to visit.

'Good-day to you,' said Dan, raising his hat and speaking with that unconventional courtesy of manner that a wild solitary life (strange as it may seem) generally produces. 'My wife will take your coming as very neighbourly, ma'm.'

I hope I am not a snob, but I was thinking of the old country, and felt there was something very comic about this simple speech.

My young friend fell to chatting with Dan and chaffing the little half-castes, while I went in to see the lady of the house and be introduced to the newcomer, whom I professed to be charmed with, like a humbug as I am; for it was a hideous little red thing, and I am not one of those women who admire all babies on principle. (I have since learnt to reconcile good manners with truth by always exclaiming, in an excited tone on such occasions, 'What a baby!' which may be construed any way.) However, the mother evidently considered it 'a thing of beauty and a joy for ever,' and I thought it kind not to unsettle her mind by doubts.

Soon after I adjourned to the other room (there were only two), where I found my young friend sacrilegiously unpacking my bundle before the eyes of the grateful Dan. It was a comfortless-looking apartment: the furniture consisted of a rough-hewn form, a rougher table, and a rickety chair; in one corner were a few axes, in another a gun, some fish-spears, and a coil of rope; in a third a confused heap of blankets, which, I rightly conjectured, formed at nighttime the beds of the rising generation of Stringers. On the wooden walls were nailed some illustrations from the *London News,* and on one side a plank, supported by cords, formed a practical, if not ornamental, bookshelf. Obeying the impulse which always takes possession of me on entering a room for the first time, I ran my eye over its much-used, threadbare-looking contents. I am quite sure that no one who knows not wild life would guess what manner of books I saw. First came Paley's *Evidences,* leaning as much away as it could from its neighbour, Paine's *Rights of Man.* Between that and *Midshipman Easy,* standing primly upright and regarding neither, was a *Polite Letter-writer* of the year seventeen hundred and something, looking, in spite of its great age, far better preserved than its neighbours; on account, I suppose, of its cool, unexcitable temperament. Then came an odd volume or two of Macaulay, *Chambers's Information for the People*, Mill's *Logic*, and a tattered backless *Pilgrim's Progress*. Huddling close together in a corner I found *The Vestiges of Creation*, and Darwin's *Descent of Man*, the constitution of the latter, in spite of its youth, evidently giving way from overwork.

It is not to be imagined, from this curious library, that our friend Dan was out of the way in his tastes for a man of his class. In many of the rough settlers' huts, in out-of-the-way parts, you will find the same kind of solid literature. Whenever they come to my house to borrow books, as they often do, I always notice that they pick out the very stiffest reading (from our view of the tastes of uneducated men) they can lay hands on; on the principle, I suppose, that made the man prefer tough beefsteaks to tender ones, because they took so much longer to eat. And the amount both of thought-pegs and reflective power they will, aided by the solitude of their life, develop out of some really worthy book, is quite astounding to more civilised beings, who drive one book through their head after another until they wear a smooth hole, incapable of retaining permanently anything that passes through it. 'You see,' said one of these settlers to me (an old Scotchman)[1] 'it's my opinion that there are some

---

[1] As I am trying to write the English language, my readers will be pleased to translate this speech into Scotch for themselves.

books that you can never derive full benefit from unless you spend almost as much time in reading them as the author did in writing; for how else are you to learn for yourself the different ramifications of thought that ended finally in the sentence you see before your eyes? It's but reading a fraction of the work to see but the sentences without the thoughts that shaped them; and not only do you thus learn to read the very mind of the author as he pored over his manuscript, but to strike out new thought-tracks for yourself, thus finding out the great secret of reading in order to think, instead of merely striving to cram an empty skull with a lot of ideas as disconnected as the words of a dictionary. Now (so said this impertinent old person), you aristocrats, who have all the advantages of education that God, man, and the Devil can give you, go gabbling through book after book, just like a man continuously taking one medicine on top of another, and never giving any of them time to take effect on his constitution. And what's the consequence? Why, after a whole lifetime of reading, you have nothing in your head but a vague jumble of other people's ideas, and seldom speak out a sentence worth listening to, because the poor creature don't know how it was born, not being developed by a systematic chain of thought, as it should be.'

He was a rude, conceited, dogmatic old person, but I felt that there was a certain amount of truth in what he said, and understood better than before what it was that so often made these rough, wild, solitary settlers such charming companions.

I knew one man, inhabiting the wild Great Banier island, who had studied natural history to such purpose that even his little children knew the name and the family of every plant in the bush with a correctness that was almost uncanny.

'Well, Dan,' said I, sipping tea out of a tin mug, 'I suppose we ought to congratulate you on this addition to your family?'

Dan's honest face clouded over, and after a pause he apparently determined to relieve his mind, for he said, hesitatingly, 'Well, you see, she never took any liking to my brats—which was my purpose in marrying her—and now she's got one of her own, I'm thinking it'll be worse.'

'So you married for the sake of the children?'

'That's just where it was, ma'm, and a bl—I beg your pardon—a terrible mess I made of it. You see, for a year or two after my old woman died, we all worried along easy enough. I was a regular savage, and had no thought of eddicating beyond teaching Johnny and Tommy to split shingles. But then, you see, after a time he (nodding towards my young friend) crammed a lot of stuff into my head, and made me feel I wanted to teach them something, as it were. And then you see, my lass, Mary, what's now at school in Auckland, grew into a woman almost, and was as flighty as a hawk. So I made up my mind for a stiff bout, and began to try and teach 'em. Well, I made about the foolishest awkwardest job of it you ever see. Maybe it was I didn't know how to set about it, maybe I began too late with them, maybe both; but my teachings always ended the same way: Mary laughing at me, Tommy howling at one end of this old bench, and Johnny sobbing at the other. You had learnt 'em just to read and write at your school, so the ground seemed to be all ready cleared for sowing, one would think. Well, I tried 'em with every book you see on that shelf, but the little rascals never took the smallest interest in anything, barring the fights in the Old Testament and the *Pilgrim's Progress*. And here I used to sit, wrastling with the long words, sometimes they mastering, sometimes I, till the sweat ran down my nose on to the paper, while they went to sleep or looked out of the window. I used to begin gently enough, but gradually get more and more riled at their pig-headed laziness, until it ended in my boxing their ears and going off with an axe to my work, with a face like a deformed potato. And then I used to chop and sweat, and sweat and chop like fury, until I got right again; for there's nothing raises a man's spirits like doing some work that he feels he *can* do.

'Things went on much the same, and I grew more and more desponding, until there came a day when no amount of sweating and chopping would bring me round. I had picked out a tree that would have raised any man's spirits, a good old tough, cross-grained *pohutikawa*, that might have turned the edge of a Harchangel's sword; but though I worked away till I could scarcely stand or see, it was no use. So I sat down, and bathed my head and arms in the sea and tried to think. I watched a little kingfisher[1] make five or six bad shots at the small fry, and almost grinned to think he was in the same lot as myself; but he nailed one the next shot, so I heaved a rock at him. And all the while, something kept whispering to me, "It's no use, Dan; you've done your best, but nature made you for the purpose of chopping wood and not of eddicating brats. You'll never make any hand of it; not if you live till ninety. You stick to woodcutting." So the long and short of it is, that by that night my mind was made up, and hearing that an emigrant ship had just arrived in Auckland, I took my passage in the *Sovereign of the Seas* cutter and married the first decent-looking lass I came athwart of.'

'Rather a rash way of doing things, that?' said my young friend, smiling.

'Lord bless you,' replied Dan, simply, 'what was the use of a man like me trying to pick and choose? I'd be as like to get hold of the wrong sow last as first.'

'How did you manage to win her affections so quickly, Dan? The recipe's worth knowing.'

[1] Kingfishers are the greatest duffers in piscatorial matters of all water-birds.

'Oh, that was simple enough,' replied he. 'The first night I arrived at the lodging-house, in Auckland, I found myself sitting next to a young woman at supper, who I soon found was one of the newly-arrived emigrants. I looked her over, and saw she was a round, strong, cheery-looking lass, with a laughing face, and thought she'd do. I didn't know how to go foolin' around her to find a soft place (as you would have done, sir, no offence to you), but just spoke a word or two with her, and when we came out into the passage gave her a squeeze and a kiss. Says she, "How dare you?" Says I, "I wants to marry you, my dear."—"Marry me!" cried she, laughing; "why, I don't know you."—"No more do I you, my dear," says I, "so that makes it all fair and equal." She didn't know how to put a clapper on that, so she only laughed and said she couldn't think of it. "Not think of it," says I, artful like, "not when you've come all these thousands of miles for the purpose?"—"What do you mean?" says she, staring. "Come, now," says I, "don't tell me. I knows what's what. When a man immigrationises, it's to get work; when a woman immigrationises, it's to get married. You may as well do it at once." Well, she giggled a bit, and we were spliced two days afterwards.'

'Well?' said I, as he concluded.

'Well,' said he, 'it was a mistaken speculation as to the purpose intended. She never took to the brats, nor the brats to her. If they had been moody or ailin', she might ha' took to 'em, woman-like; but with such wild undependent little rascals, she never had no call.'

Soon after this we started home. Night had come on, but the moon shone out brightly, and we scrambled down to the boat without any accident, and glided slowly down the little creek into the mangrove swamp. It was high tide, so that at times we were floating over the very tops of the trees. In shallower places the glasslike smoothness of the water, and the intense white light, caused a perfect reflection of their weird forms beneath them, making them look (as one could not distinguish the water-line) as if they had been dragged up from the soil and balanced on the tips of their roots on the bosom of the smooth sea. The stillness was almost oppressive, and it seemed as though the sound of the oars would have reached miles on miles. The cry of a 'more pork' in a distant gully sounded close in our ears. We crept along slowly and cautiously for fear of snags, the hideous mangroves stretching out their contorted limbs toward us, the harbour before us looking like a milky sheet, contrasting strangely with the black hills that surrounded it, until we gained open water once more and shot away towards home.

'There is no Arcadia,' said my young friend, with a half laugh. 'You rush to the wilderness to escape the evils connected with human life (and, as you think, civilisation), and there you find the same miseries, jealousies, heartburnings, and skeletons-in-the-closet generally, exactly the same. The same! the same! even to the woman's stays. Did you see Mrs. Stringer's hanging up behind the door? I hate stays.

'I came out into the wilderness,' continued he, dreamily, 'because I found myself utterly alone amongst men—with them, but not of them in any way. They all seemed to me to be incapable of judging anything from a broad, distant standpoint, to require a year or two's residence in another planet to teach them to look at their world and its affairs as a whole from outside. I felt myself painfully

> '"Like the poor ghost of some man lately dead,
> That's had but time the lesson to have read,
> That all his earthly faith was not correct,
> That God is not the leader of a sect,
> Is something different from a perfect man,—
> Then is sent back to shift as best it can,
> In its old world, and live among a race,
> Each damning each, and all assured of grace;
> Where every creed declares it's wholly right,
> And swears it has a patent for God's light."

It is a very hard fate to be cursed with an eccentric way of thinking. Wherever I go, amongst Christians, Mohammedans, Buddhists, Hindus, or cannibals, I am in the same position—an outcast from all sympathy. I flee into the bush, and, behold! both literally and metaphorically, I find stays!'

'Mrs. Stringer ought to have those stays

preserved in the family archives after this,' said I, laughing. 'But don't despond, my dear boy, though I know your position is a hard one to bear. For you may be sure that a fair, liberal way of thinking has a good influence on those about you, though neither you nor they may be conscious of it :

> '"Good cheer, faint heart! Though all look dark,
> Though few men know, each leaves his mark.
> So each must struggle, straight and stark,
>   In this world's great fraternity.
> For every passing glimpse of thought,
> Fleeting, perhaps, and scarcely caught,
> Shows where some battle's being fought,
>   A landmark in Eternity."'

And so we rowed home.

CHAPTER IV

WE hear, see, and read so much nowadays about cruel deceivers and false friends, that it is rather strange that none of the great thinkers or inventors of the day have devoted their talents to the discovery of some tests by which the depth and nature of friendships may be ascertained. Simple observation has taught me one, and I here give my valuable recipe to the world gratis.

Take two so-called friends, and place them in some silent spot on two chairs, not less than two yards (three if male and female) nor more than five yards apart. Place in the hands of each a tolerably amusing book, and retire to some hiding-place to watch their proceedings. Of course an enormous deal will always depend upon the weather, character, and temper; but I think one may lay down a few general rules :—

1. If they shut up the books at once and begin to *make conversation* to each other, you may surmise that the friendship is only cutting its teeth. 2. If they try to read for a longer or

shorter period, glancing at their books with an evident consciousness of each other's presence till they can bear it no longer, you may decide that the friendship has gone into jackets and trousers. 3. If they throw down the books at once and talk eagerly to each other, taking an evident pleasure both in speaking, listening, and watching, you are justified in thinking that the friendship has reached the period of its poetical youth. 4. But if the two sit down and read away contented and happy for hour after hour, as if each was a stock or stone, you may be pretty sure that you are gazing at two lucky souls in whom perfect love and familiar knowledge have cast out all fear, all self-consciousness, all anxiety, all curiosity, all feverishness whatsoever.

Which reflections were brought into my head by a consideration of the extremely unsociable manner in which my young friend and I had spent the last hour and a half.

It was a fiery-hot day—dead calm—so, giving ourselves up recklessly to the goddess of laziness, we had sculled the dingey under the pleasant shade of a vast overhanging tree, and had there remained, studying our books and occasionally glimmering through the network of branches at the blinding glare outside. He sat at one end of the boat, I at the other, like a couple of children playing see-saw. His attire was certainly careless. He had been fishing under the fierce sun till even his well-seasoned skin had peeled off from his face, neck, and arms, forcing him to arrange his shirt-front and collar in a kind of demi-toilette fashion to avoid friction. I am aware that this description is very nasty, but it is such a marked feature of colonial skins that I cannot bring myself to cut it out. His feet were dabbling in the water, and he was doubled up over his book as though he was trying to bring his whole body to bear on it instead of only his head. And his abstraction was not to be wondered at, for the book he was studying was Charles Kingsley's *Alton Locke*, a work which, in spite of its *soupçon* of want of finish, is undeniably marked by a power and a grim earnestness which must always make it interesting to any thoughtful reader. Besides which, though Charlie had a mind too eccentric and strongly-marked to worship any writer with blind faith, he certainly contrived to worship Charles Kingsley to a degree that was almost absurd; a fact which I wish to impress on the minds of my readers, lest the following conversation should be misunderstood. He used to declare that he was the greatest combination of the poet and the novelist, the humorist and the tear-drawer, of our day, excepting, perhaps, Bulwer Lytton; that he had, besides, a fresh, pure, noble manliness peculiarly his own, and appearing, in all that he wrote, that made the study of one of his novels seem like the breath of a bright sea-breeze on a sultry day. And yet, as the reader may guess, there were very few points on which he and Charles Kingsley could cordially agree. I could not help, in my shallowness, hinting this to him one day, adding, that if his idol ever came across either him or his opinions, he (the idol) would probably call both some hard names, which would be very unpleasant to read or listen to. At which my young friend laughed a great laugh, saying, 'Well, I shouldn't like him any the worse if he did. It's not his creed or opinions that I admire so fiercely, but the man as I see him in his books—not the way the spirit works, but the spirit itself. If he suddenly took it into his head to swear the moon was made of green cheese, and that the whole world would be damned for not believing it, it would scarcely alter my feeling about him, because it could scarcely touch the rather indefinable something in him that I admire. I tell you, that supposing his philosophy was utter rubbish, that all his thoughts were based upon fallacies, that his knowledge of human nature was utterly mistaken—which things are not so, as it happens—his works would still do men more good than the most logical, sensible, undeniable wisdom and truth of any cold-blooded philosopher; because the pure, bright, fearless manliness that is, I think, the key to their charm, would still be there. When I meet a soul wholesome and decided, without being thought-fearing or shallow, earnest, and living without being unpractical or useless from hesitation, I take off my hat to it and bow my knee, though it may hold the opinions of the Pope of Rome or the Delhi-Lama of Thibet.

'For, after all, these brain-maggots called opinions are merely the accessory trappings of that one important and beautiful thing—a conscientious, truth-loving heart.

'We all feel that our consciences are meant to be our guides, and that it is our duty to seek truth with them, and that they will not altogether lead us wrong. Won't they? cry you. How then do you account for all the conscientious truth-seekers running into various directions and crashing fiercely against each other? I reply, that most likely they are building God's palace of truth by so doing. At least we may trust *that* to Him.

> '" Soul against soul in life's short span
> We strive, yet only work this plan —
> He that made each and every man,
>   Not scorning a minority,
> Glory in pain—respect to foe—
> And shame on rancour whilst we know
> That each man works and strikes his blow,
>   With God for his authority."

'No! When we find the true metal, don't let us be too fastidious about the shape of it. Hang opinions, if the soul they are grown on is of the right kind. It is the most earnest, most honest man, rather than the most acute, that does God's work in the world. In short, whatever folly Charles Kingsley might write or believe, my admiration would not give way, for he would still be the man who wrote *and felt.*

> ' " Be earnest, earnest, earnest—mad, if thou wilt ;
> Do what thou dost as if the stake were heaven,
> And that thy last deed ere the judgment day—" '

Now, whether my young friend was right or wrong in this audacious tirade, I cannot give an opinion ; but it struck me at the moment that if the youth of the present day could catch a little of his enthusiastic, objection-swallowing admiration for that peculiar, fearless, fresh, manly earnestness depicted in and by Charles Kingsley, it would do them enormous good, and tend to make the life of the coming generation something better and nobler than the history of fashions and cant opinions that it promises to be. 'For,' Charlie used to say, ' the great rushes of cant opinions and principles so common nowadays on every subject and of every sort, though they are born of a tendency to thought, are caused by shallowness and carelessness in thinking.' But I am wandering away ; let us get back to the boat under the big tree.

I had lifted my eyes from my book to indulge in a reverie, and then, it having come to an end, leaving me on the highest pinnacle of glory or weeping over my own untimely death—I forget which—I took to watching the expression of my young friend's face, and trying to guess his reflections as he read.

His countenance was impassible ; but soon he

began to sniff and grunt occasionally, not like a pleased pig, but like an offended pig grunts; till at last he threw down the book into the bottom of the boat, saying, 'What a pity the finishes of both this book and *Yeast* are such failures; they are so horribly disappointing.'

'How so?' asked I.

'Well,' replied he, 'all through the first parts the author's appreciation and thorough knowledge of doubts and difficulties lead one to expect a great deal at the conclusion. When a sceptic gets hold of one of these books, he is filled at first with wonder and admiration at seeing his own side of the question so fairly and so forcibly stated. Even where its weaknesses are attacked, the assault is so fair and undeniable that he feels none of the irritation that most sneers at the different speculations of thought cause him. For instance, that chapter which contains the Deist sermon, and Sandy Mackaye's sarcastic comments thereon, is not only the wittiest, but perhaps the fairest and truest compressed sketch of Deism and its shortcomings that has ever been written. And the delighted sceptic cries, "Here is a man who understands the force of our difficulties, and does not misrepresent them either to himself or the public," and reads on eagerly, feeling certain that he is going at last to see a clear, logical drawing of the path by which an honest thinker may march back from his sea of doubts into a positive belief in the doctrines of Christianity. But when the time for converting the freethinker arrives, behold the whole chain of clear, honest thinking that runs through the book suddenly cut off, two or three rather abstruse rhapsodies poured in, some noble religious person thrust prominently forward, and hi presto! the freethinker is turned into a Christian, the whole of his doubts and their possible solutions as utterly ignored as if they had never been, while the unfortunate sceptic who has been reading for edification finds himself suddenly left out in the cold miles behind, wondering how on earth the marvellous transformation is effected!'

I reply exasperatingly, 'Of course, it is much easier to attack than to answer an attack—to pull down than to build up,' being perfectly aware in my own heart that this impregnable statement is not the least to the point. He glares at me vindictively for a moment and then remarks quietly, 'I cut my last tooth at least three weeks ago, and firmly believe, moreover, that there *are* milestones on the Dover road.'

There was a long pause. 'Perhaps,' said I, gravely, 'he believes, like many others, that God often leads men to religion by other means than their mere intellect.'

'I should be a fool to doubt it,' replied he, rather drily, 'with the evidence of probably ninety-nine hundredths of mankind before me to prove it. I don't think I have ever had a talk with you without harping on the subject of spiritual yearnings and vacancies in the human mind almost to weariness, and shall have to say more yet. At this moment I will only suggest, that though it is not for me or any one to lay down the law as to how far, what way, and when God influences men's minds, we should, instead of hastily denominating these inclinations, " Supernatural Calls," look into our minds carefully, and try to find out what feelings produce them.

'I don't speak altogether in ignorance of such things, for I have felt them often and terribly. Some men will say that I have received angels unawares, and scorned them; but to me they seemed devils in disguise, attempting, by means of my cowardly dislike to the acceptance of unpleasant convictions, and my want of trust in the power that made me, to tamper with the honesty of my thought and conscience.

'But this question of spiritual longings, etc., and my way of looking upon them, is only a secondary part of the wide divergence of thought that makes the method of conversion implied in *Yeast*, *Alton Locke*, the last few words of *Two Years Ago*, and many books by various authors, so utterly incomprehensible or intangible to the true sceptic. I refer to the question as to the identity or relationship of absolute truth and utility—of what is most probably true, and what it is best, pleasantest, or wisest for men to believe.

'The sceptic holds them to be separate, and his reasons may be briefly summed up in these words—" I see in this day all kinds of contradictory opinions and dogmas all over the world, working enormous good to those who hold them."

'Being an honest man, I can neither shut my eyes to their utility, nor the fact that, as they all differ and contradict each other, a great proportion of them must be, and probably all are, untrue. I look back on the history of the world, and again see the flat denial of the theory that what is good for men to believe in must be true, or *vice versâ*. I see a whole string of opinions, doctrines, and creeds doing good in their day, then knocked away as false, useless, or bad, to be replaced by others more suited to the state of mental progress (*and consequently the spiritual wants of men*). And this leads me to believe, not only that truth and utility are not and have not been identical, but that they cannot be so until the time that man arrives at perfection; since man's capability both to understand and appreciate real truth would necessarily imply that progress was at an end.

'This mental position of the sceptics—of which I will only say, in passing, that it takes a deal of that contemptible science, "word-frittering," to destroy it—makes the form of conversion practised in the books before mentioned utterly unintelligible to him. What on earth had Tom's being unable to get out of prison got to do with his doubts about the theory of the fall of man, or the reality of eternal damnation? He feels that the writer is utterly off the line somehow, and that there is some gulf fixed between them. They are playing at cross purposes, and the key to it is the mental position above sketched. When the writer (I am not making Charles Kingsley in particular my dummy to bolster) effects the conversion of his freethinker by tacitly ignoring his previous doubts, and making him realise the soul-satisfying powers, the splendid moral guidance, the glorious working effects of religion, the sceptic who reads shuts up the book in despair, crying, "My dear Sir, why suddenly leave the thinking and doubting *in medias res*, and branch off to expatiate on a subject on which we are perfectly agreed, and which does not touch upon our difficulties in any way?" I know as well as you the utility of your religion; I appreciate as thoroughly as you *can* do its wonderful suitability to mankind in its present stage; but so far from that being an argument in favour of its probable *truth*, it seems to me a very strong argument against it. What is the use of saying to me, "See how well this works!" I know how well it works as well as you do—the peculiar fitness of its several dogmas to the spiritual wants of men *as they are at present* is one of my favourite studies; but what has this to do with my doubts concerning its theories about things beyond the reach of human knowledge? The fact that it has, on the whole, a very good influence on men's thoughts and actions, does not make it a bit easier for me to believe that a just and merciful God (*sic*) created millions of human beings with a destiny of misery, or that He, being omnipotent, wages war with the Devil for the human souls He brought into existence, and so on.'

'I suppose,' said I, 'that he would say that a tree was to be known by its fruits?'

'Confusion again,' replied he; 'for of course there we agree up to a certain point. From seeing the works of a religion I see it is a good one; from tasting figs I know the fig-tree to be a good tree; but if figs were the best fruit in the world, I should not declare that the fig-tree was a perfect and supernatural tree, while the rest of the vegetable kingdom was imperfect and natural; I should only remark that figs were admirably adapted to the palate of man.'

'But,' said I, 'the effect of Christianity on men's minds is so much greater and better than that produced by any other religion.'

'The difference is only one of degree,' was the answer; 'and it seems to me absurd to call a horse supernatural, and a donkey mere earthly dust, because the horse gallops rather better than the donkey. Besides, please remember that the sceptic, from his point of view, would say that your statement only went to show the superior suitability of Christianity to the state of the human mind, and did not touch on the question of *Divine*[1] truth in any way.'

---

[1] As I am fully aware that nearly all the speculations contained in these chapters may be turned into utter nonsense by a system of

'Does God then use lies in doing His work?' asked I, gravely, with a feeling of repulsion.

'Look round,' said he, with that strange solemnity which (in spite of the quaintness of his language) always came over him when talking of what he called 'the great mysteries,' 'and see the good that false creeds and utterly contradictory opinions are working. Look back and see what good false convictions, you may call them lies if you please, have done in their time—false convictions which have not only developed into something better, but been actually knocked away as wrong and pernicious, when mankind has outgrown them. My dear soul, though I hold it wrong to make theories about God which must lead to contradictions and blasphemy, it does not follow that I think that we should close the eyes and the minds He has given us to this or that, because it will not harmonise with the notions we choose to hold about Him and His ways. If once we give way to this, we soon find ourselves, in order to understand His plan, doing the very thing I think most wrong; that is to say—

"" Make God a man like us—create a Devil,
  And drag our creed down to a human level."

But to go back to our subject: I wanted to show how the author of *Yeast*, *Alton Locke*, etc., though he certainly has studied the freethinking

judicious quibbling on the meaning of the word '*truth*,' I wish to state once for all that whenever it is used in these pages it is used in its fullest and most quibble-despising sense.

writers far more widely and constantly than I have done, has contrived to make the moral of his books useless to real sceptics from an omission of one of their most important principles.'

And then we pondered in silence for awhile.

There is no doubt that my young friend was a very giddifying person to talk to. When a person at one moment fiercely denounces fallacies and evasions in thought, and declares at the next that all mankind, himself of course included, cannot possibly know truth until the perfection of their race and the conclusion of progress, and that yet they must believe that the fallacies they hold are absolute truths, because if they did not the said fallacies would have no power to improve them; when he in short looks at the world as though from the outside at one minute, and from the inside at the next, it really requires a powerful effort of the brain to keep all the connecting links of his mental scheme in sight at once. Not that they were to him unconnected or contradictory;— if I have not succeeded in showing my readers this I have written in vain.

After much meditation I say at last, 'Look here! Supposing I grant that your theory that no man can know real truth till man is perfect; that all creeds are successive revelations of thought, causing and being caused by the progress of humanity; and supposing at the same time we hold (as you *do*) that Christianity is a form of opinion in every way better suited to man's state of mental progress than any we know—is the right thing at the right date? Does it not follow that the most reasonable thing to do is to be a Christian?'

'Mercy on us,' cried he, gasping; 'that's the most delightful argument I ever heard out of a pulpit. You are to start with the premises that all religions are waves of opinion and cannot be really true, and still believing this, to conclude that one of them is really true because it is the one best suited to mankind in your day. In other words—Christianity can't be true, because religions are merely successive waves of mental progress; but I am to believe it true because it is well suited to the present age. I wish you would think before you speak!'

I am silent and confounded, being conscious that my attempt at a bold speculation has been hardly a success. But I would tell the exasperated reader that if he has never heard an equally silly argument in a theological discussion he is a person blessed among his fellows. I am not satisfied, and continue to reflect. I cannot help thinking that if there were not two or three screws loose in his way of thinking it would lead to something more definitely useful, a point on which, I am well aware, he would utterly disagree with me.

'I think,' said I at last, 'that religious people would say that you elevated reason to the exclusion of all the other qualities of our souls. There is something more than mere reason in us. God made our spiritual cravings as well as our reason, and I suppose intended them to be satisfied quite as much as the former.'

I must trouble the reader to remember that my young friend had a firm conviction that all things were God's work and had a purpose, whether men called them false or true, good or evil, or he may find the true meaning of this sentence rather confusing.

'I never denied,' cried he, rather hotly, 'that God made our spiritual cravings as much as any other part of us, and that He intended us to satisfy them we have the evidence of nearly all mankind to prove; *but, in spite of its undoubted utility in leading men into the form of belief best suited to their temperament and character*, it is a fallacy, and a fallacy that strikes at the very root of all honest thought. God made the tips of our noses and the smalls of our backs, but they are not the right bits of us to analyse the truth or untruth of a dogma with. To say that God made our spiritual cravings as much as our reason, and that one should be considered as much as another, sounds plausible enough; but when you analyse honestly the question of judging the truth or untruth of any opinion by any other faculty than your understanding and reason, and apply it *honestly* to your own mind, you will see the utter hollowness of the plea.'[1]

---

[1] As the question as to whether utility was to be looked on as a test of truth had been already discussed, I refrained from bringing

A long pause.

'Unless,' said I, 'you hold that these spiritual cravings of your soul are divine voices, as some do.'

'Oh,' replied he, rather scornfully, 'if once you take upon yourself to decide that certain of your mental impressions are the infallible promptings of God, to the exclusion of all the rest, you make for yourself a false mental standpoint from which you can get into a clothes-basket and lift yourself up by the handle as often as you please.

'But I think that both this last assumption and the plausible theory you advanced just now are nothing more nor less than mental excuses (their dishonesty being often quite unconscious) for believing what seems to us pleasantest and best, for blindfolding our reason when it leads towards unpleasant and terrible convictions, thus changing it from an honest, truth-loving, though not an infallible guide, into an obedient, unscrupulous special pleader.'

'I don't quite see how,' said I.

'This is how. Your sweet-sounding theory is, that our spiritual desires and necessities and our reason or understanding should be equally consulted. All very fine whilst they agree; but what when they flatly contradict each other? Then it comes to this, that one or the other must

up the argument again by using that common, but from my young friend's point of view very unwarranted assumption, that the fact of anything being desirable and useful to our minds was a part proof of its actual truth.

go to the wall, and we must choose which it is to be. Here comes the real split between two great schools of thinking. "Don't be a coward," cries honest thought. "Give your conscience and your understanding free play to lead you where they will. Fear nothing, shrink from nothing, but trust God." The other voice cries, "Pause ere you cast away a belief that is so comforting, so useful, and so strengthening to your soul, whether it be true or not, at the command of your fallible reason. Force yourself to believe it, and force your reason if possible to help you to. Cling to it! Press it to your heart; and soon your reason, instead of continuing the attack, will come round to the side you wish it to." If a man listens to the first voice, he will march out into the cold a freethinker, with a terribly sore and cold heart from the wrench that has just taken place; and with this only for a reward—that he will have learnt a lesson in honest thought that will never be effaced. If he listens to the other he will have degraded his reason by teaching it a dishonourable trick *that it will never forget;* he will have planted his roots of belief in unjustifiable ground. But he will soon forget all this, if he has even ever been conscious of it, and will slide back into the pleasant fields of a dogmatic creed, will live most likely a good and useful life, helped and protected by the dreams he was so loth to cast away, and will perhaps—die a bishop.

'And so, as the theory of treating your spiritual

wants and your intellect with equal consideration is a mere fallacy—an excuse—a quibble—first, because your intellect and reason, or understanding, should be the sole unbiassed judge of the truth of anything—the admission of your inclinations and wishes as evidence being palpably fatal; secondly, because the two cannot honestly be mixed, you must choose between them. Here are the two thought-paths; the choice you make will determine the whole future of your mind. To embrace the system, which, for want of a better name, I call the freethinking one; that is, to let your reason and conscience do their work unbiassed, and to accept the convictions they lead you to, whether they be pleasant or terrible, useful or useless to you; or else to make yourself believe in those things which are pleasant and good for your soul, and use your reason to cover the falseness of your mental standpoint. The first is the way to seek truth, and nothing more; the second is death to all truth-seeking, but, on the other hand, is the safest, the pleasantest, and the most practically useful one for your soul. The latter process is really not very difficult. You have only to persuade yourself that those warning whispers, which spring from a want of courage to face terrible truths, and want of trust in God, are Divine counsels, to glorify them by the vague term of faith, and there you are.'

'You are not talking with your usual fairness,' said I; 'you know very well that there are many people who honestly believe that doubt is sin.'

'I wasn't speaking of them,' replied he, 'they are mere ingenious toys made by a certain machinery on a certain pattern, not reasoning or thinking animals properly so-called.[1] I was talking of those who have examined the place where the two paths diverge, and made their choice. And though I strive daily not to become a bigot, is it easy for a freethinker not to despise these minds? When they call their cowardice and want of trust by such a pretty name as faith, when they call their unwillingness to confess man's ignorance of supernatural things by the pretty name of humility, persuading themselves of the truth of what they say by an ingenious metamorphosis of the whole position—when they actually glory in having turned back from the battlefields that we have fought through at such a terrible cost of agony and loss of comfort—when they turn round and revile us with the very failings we despise most in them—when *they* who lay down the law about God, and His ways, and ideas, and advice to them, as if He was an intimate acquaintance, reproach us with a conceited belief in the unlimited reach of the human intellect—is it easy for us to help despising their deliberate moral perversity?

'For do you suppose that we poor devils don't

---

[1] Neither is this fair altogether; but the best of us are apt to draw in strong colours things that grate roughly on our clearest and most earnest feelings.

know what these spiritual calls and cravings are, which they place on such a lofty pedestal? The first plunge from religion into doubt is really terrible; all behind us seems so pleasant, so comforting, so utterly necessary to us—all before so hopeless, so blank, so terrible. Day and night, two voices are whispering in our ears. One soft, yet firm, saying, "You are bone of my bone, flesh of my flesh; you cannot stand without me, you will lose your way without me, and you know it; without me all is chaos. I will make you happy and good. Your love for me, which is not yet gone, shall be the glory of your life, and after your death I promise you a certain ecstasy of beatitude beyond the power of words to describe; while, if you leave me———" The other voice, calm and clear, cries again and again, "Seek truth honestly, and trust the rest to the Power that made you." Every bribe one side, *none* on the other; a stormy ocean before us, a pleasant haven behind. I tell you that first death grapple between the beliefs which have formed part of our very soul, which have influenced, or seemed to influence, our smallest actions, and the honesty of a truth-seeking conscience, are really very terrible. But the agony of it does not last very long after the first great battle. For the habit of thinking honestly, regardless of consequences, soon becomes a second nature, *and from the realisation of our blank ignorance about Divine things we learn of necessity a blind trust in God that makes us almost smile at the misery we experienced at the outset.* We march along the path of life, fearlessly following the conscience He has given us as honestly as we can, feeling that, in a great trust, we have found peace, though not the peace of sleep.'

There was a pause; and then, in a grave, quiet voice, he repeated the first two verses of Doctor Newman's beautiful hymn—

> ' Lead, kindly light, amid the encircling gloom,
>   Lead thou me on;
> The night is dark, and I am far from home;
>   Lead thou me on.
> Keep thou my feet—I do not ask to see
> The distant scene—one step enough for me.
>
> ' I was not ever thus, nor pray'd that thou
>   Should'st lead me on;
> I loved to choose, and see my path—but now
>   Lead thou me on.
> I loved the garish day; and spite of fears,
> Pride ruled my will—remember not past years.'

' The author would be a little astonished,' remarked I, trying to lighten the rather oppressive solemnity of our conversation, ' to hear his words in the mouth of a fatalist and a freethinker.'

' Would he?' replied Charlie. ' *Les extrêmes se touchent.*' You know there is not a word in those verses that does not fit exactly the feelings of a freethinker who has passed through the great conflict, and has found the calmer water beyond. Having been taught to think he knew what never can be known, he has thrown his false claims to knowledge to the winds, and humbled himself in a terrible confession of ignorance; and then he follows the light that God has given him, wheresoever it pleases to lead him, learning a complete trust from the very intensity of the darkness, and gaining from that trust a humble but serene and fearless heart.'

'I can't help thinking still,' said I, 'that you are really unfair to those who allow their spiritual cravings or intuitions, as I suppose they would call them, to outweigh their reason. You have no right to assume that they are consciously dishonest.'

'Knock out the word "intuitions," if you please, because calling these cravings "intuitions" in the sense they mean, is part of the dishonesty of thought that I am attacking. Perhaps I am rather unfair; they at least do not set me a good example, for there is no class of minds on earth that more bitterly hates, and persistently misrepresents, the simple spade-is-a-spade freethinker, than the gang of ingenious acrobats who gambol on the edge of the Rubicon of Thought.

'You see it is really very difficult for a freethinker to conceive that they can allow their judgment on the truth or untruth of a question to be biassed by their spiritual inclinations or wants, without being conscious, if only for a moment, of dishonesty of thought. That this mode of analysis and speculation is dishonest, whether those who accept it are conscious of the fact or not, that it is as great an enemy to truth as it is a friend to practical utility, I have no hesitation in affirming. You see there are several reasons besides those I have mentioned that make it very difficult for a freethinker to abstain from bitterness on the subject of this " root." For the spiritually self-indulgent (and I hold) the false path *is* so very pleasant; while the other, for the first period at least, is so extremely blank and wretched. You must own it is exasperating to hear your friend, who has just looked at the cold water and then sat himself down on the bank and wrapped himself up in the warm blanket of faith, as you fain would do, calling you names whilst you are battling, sorely against your inclinations, with the icy stream, for not having stopped on the bank like himself. Again, as I said before, once you have taught your reason a dishonest trick, it will never forget it; from this one bit of dishonest thinking at the root comes a whole chain of fallacies, producing, amongst others, one series of pictures that no true freethinker can look at without shame and sorrow—that of great minds trying obstinately with clouds of ingenious sophistry to prove the truth of opinions which the veriest child can perceive are utterly unwarranted when they are placed naked before his eyes. Mind! I don't mean to accuse these people of conscious dishonesty in so speaking or writing; if there was any conscious dishonesty at the first choosing of the path, it has long since been forgotten; but their judgment and reason have become the slaves instead of the masters of their minds, and unbiassed honesty of thought is gone from them for ever. One cannot be exactly angry with them, because their dishonesty is so completely unconscious; but they give one a kind of hopeless, bewildered feeling, that makes one wonder whether all thinking is not mere useless vexation of spirit.

'And the worst of it is that the unfair, dishonest system of thought, of which that split between possible truth and the soul's needs is the true root, however remote, affects the minds that are naturally honest and truth-loving almost as much as those that are naturally shifty. To the freethinker they seem as though one of their eyes, though able to see, had no brain behind it to realise what it saw. If he talks with them, he is in a state of perpetual confusion and astonishment, for they will scarcely accept any evidence that does not point in the direction they like.

'Only the other day I was talking with that dear old Papist M——, the judge, who, as you know, is one of the truest old souls that ever lived. I was arguing that the doctrines of the New Testament were essentially—nay, horribly—damnatory, and he was opposing me. I asked him if Christ Himself was not reported to have said, that he that believed in Him would be saved, and that he that did not believe would be damned. Whereon he expatiated for ten minutes on the meanings of the word "belief," then ten minutes more on the meanings of the word "saved," and then at least a quarter of an hour on the meaning of "damnation," till he had proved to his own satisfaction that either the sentence meant nothing at all, or what he chose it to mean. When I, utterly exhausted with my attempts to follow him through his mazes of sophistry, remonstrated wildly against this unceremonious burking of a plain sentence, he replied calmly that there was nothing so fallacious as taking words merely in their superficial sense, and catching at hasty generalisations—a remark about as true and as much to the point as a statement that a cannon is a more useful implement of war on the field of battle than a coal-scuttle. Of course I gave in— it was sheer waste of time arguing with a mind in such a state; but I reflected, that if the sentence quoted had told against my argument as strongly as it did against his, I, or any real freethinker, would have bitten our tongues out with shame before we could have brought ourselves to quibble away its meaning in that fashion. Do you see now the reasons why I hate the mental fallacy of consulting your spiritual necessities on the question of truth? The root is, "I must believe these things true; and these things are true, because they are necessary to my soul." From that comes "these things are true, whether reason is reconciled to them or not; but we will reconcile our reason;" —what honest thought can come out of such a Nazareth as that?'

'Have you any more reasons for hating these

unfortunates?' asked I, rather crossly; for the weather was very hot, and I was not altogether pleased with my young friend's unusual intemperance of feeling.

'I will sum up my reasons for detesting them in one sentence,' replied he. 'Though they are really renegades from the cause of honest truth-seeking, they claim to be not only truthseekers, but truthfinders.'

'The world seems to be in a hopeless way,' sneered I, 'with such a very small leaven of the freethinking elect in it. Upon my word, you are getting dreadfully bumptious. I begin to doubt, after all, whether you are any better than the crowd of shallow young reformers who rave perpetually against intolerance and onesidedness, and are themselves as intolerant and onesided as men can be.'

He flushed to the very roots of his hair, set his mouth and his brows, and looked so thoroughly furious for a moment that I wished that I had been struck dumb before making such a speech. I felt too that the sneer was only half fair,[1] and that I should have remembered that to call a man, whose whole creed in life is tolerance and honesty of thought, intolerant or partial, is really as bitter and terrible an insult as to give an honourable man the lie direct to his face. A continued ex-

[1] It was of the same order as that delightful paradox which calls hatred of intolerance—intolerance; which I can honestly recommend to the reader as a true weapon wherewith to drive his freethinking acquaintances into a mixture of idiocy and frenzy.

perience of such bitter words from bitterer lips than mine had trained him, however, to force his temper under, if only for the purpose of giving his brains fair play. So he answered in a rather metallic voice, which softened as it went on: 'From a stranger who had been listening to the last half-hour's conversation, that sneer would have been excusable; but from you, who know that I always divide these questions into two parts—their relation to truth-seeking and their practical utility—it can only be pardoned in consideration of the heat of the weather. Hitherto I have merely been considering a thought-path as it affected truth-seeking, therefore your insinuation that I presume to think the world in a bad way because of the small number of freethinkers is absurd, as such considerations come under the subject of the utility of the thought-path, which I have not yet touched upon.'

'Don't bring out an elephant to fight a butterfly,' pleaded I. 'You are so dreadfully savage against a thoughtless speech.'

'Because,' said he, laughing, 'the consciousness of the beam in my own eye,[1] which I am always striving to pull out, makes me supernaturally conscious of the mote in other people's. But to go back to our subject. I am not going to give an opinion as to whether there are too many or

---

[1] My young friend had a theory that no man *could* thoroughly perceive and appreciate a fault in his neighbour that he did not to a certain degree possess himself—a maddening speculation!

too few freethinkers in the world, because I believe God's combinations of antagonistic forces *must* be correct, or, in other words, "whatever is, is right," a doctrine which, though it shocks people by admitting the necessary existence of what we call evil, also *justifies the struggles that tend to its gradual extinction.* He will take care that the sum is correct in the end, which is no business of ours. But there is nothing wrong in trying to see *how* He is working, and the thought-path we have been talking of, the principle (which I firmly believe false as regards truth-seeking) of allowing our spiritual wants to bias our judgment, seems to me one of the most ingenious and simple of His methods of leading mankind towards improvement. For, by allowing his spiritual cravings to affect his judgment, a man naturally falls into the belief best suited to his temperament, character, and the shape of his mind. Absolute truth and utility are not the same thing, as I am always saying. Mankind must go through phase after phase of belief and opinion in its own onward march, and this law, which tends to invest each individual with the phase best suited to bring out his energies, is as beautiful as it is simple. It is this wise and salutary law (fallacy though the thought-path be) that makes it fortunately so nearly impossible to convert a religious man into a sceptic by any amount of reasoning, and that is indeed the way to the much-talked-of " Missionary failure." It is *impossible to effect the conversion of a race unless they have at least partially outgrown the religion they profess;* and if missionaries would acknowledge this fact, and examine how far the standards of the religions they are trying to subvert are suited to the mental and moral stages of the races, instead of abusing the Devil, and white traders, as the cause of their failure, we should soon possess a more scientific knowledge of the keys to the durability of religions and the mental roots of races than we have at present. I should like to get hold of the statistics of the number of the men who have been converted from a lower faith to a higher by spiritual cravings, and compare it with the number that have been converted by simple reason. I fear poor reason would not have many talents to show.'

'Look!' cried he; and peering over the side of the boat into the clear, dark water, I saw a glorious yellowtail lying motionless, with his back almost touching the bottom of the dingey. He must have weighed full forty pounds. This affection of theirs for a boat is really curious. They will accompany one for miles and miles, gamboling round it occasionally, but generally keeping their post steadily under its keel. When the boat stops they will stop too; and peering over its side, you will see the splendid green and gold phantom waiting as still and patient as fate for the next movement, until you begin to feel a superstitious shudder. If you approach a floating log, you will generally find a whole shoal of these mysterious and beautiful fish worshipping it as though it were a fetish. Fortunately for the yellowtail, there were no fishing-granes in the boat, so he was allowed to dream and speculate in peace. I use the words advisedly, for I never could see a yellowtail under a boat without wondering what he thought of it.

'Tell me,' said I, after a while, 'something that puzzles me about you. You say, in the first place, that nothing exists that has not a purpose. But you always talk of yourself and your school as though you were so utterly out of joint with the times as to be practically useless, if not actually mischievous. You are continually stating that you see the beauty and use of the yokes you cannot force your neck under ; you are continually declaiming the uselessness of your creed to humanity — yourself included — as it exists at present, and almost exulting in the fact that it is so much out of joint with the times that men won't have it. Do you consider that you or those like you have a place and use in the world, or that you were pitched into it at the wrong time by an unfortunate mistake?'

He laughed rather sadly. 'Oh no! we have got our place and use like the rest. You may look on us as experiments—or prophecies of new revolutions of opinions. We are the blossoms that the plant shoots forth too early in the spring, so unfitted for the temperature as to be apparently wasted, yet typifying the fruit and flowers that are to come. And indirectly we are a useful enough ingredient in the sea of thoughts and deeds. We are the wooden spoons that keep the practical porridge from stagnating. We are a living protest against narrow-mindedness, sluggishness, and intolerant uniformity of thought. For the progress of mankind is not that of a battalion advancing in an even line, but a great, scattered, confused crowd marching, some slowly, some fast, in the same direction. Some straggle behind and are lost, some rush too far to the front and are lost too, while the great seething mass in the middle march slowly onwards, *their pace being regulated greatly by those behind and in front.* And though those in front rush so far ahead as to fall into quagmires and ambuscades; though they find themselves continually in deserts and defiles which scarcely they, still less the mass behind them, can pass through without destruction until they are better equipped; though, from being so far removed from the rest, they are continually liable to be cut off helpless and useless; they are *not* without their use, for by their example and their voice they are continually filling the minds of their comrades with a feeling that the time for halting and sleeping is not yet come. Call them foolhardy in their courage if you will—their foolhardiness does good.

'And don't, for Heaven's sake,' continued he, 'fancy that because I happen to believe that we are ahead of the mass of human opinion, I consider it anything to be conceited about. For it is a mere matter of accident, or rather destiny, after all. The balance and mixture of conscience and temperament lead one man in one direction, and his brother, *almost* perhaps his *fac-simile*, in another. I have no right to say my neighbour is not conscientious because his conscience points him out softer walls to bang his head against than mine.

'My mixture of conscience and temperament have led me in one direction, and here I am : I can only say " Kismet !" and do my best ; but so far from being proud of any part of my position except its honesty, I am daily lamenting that my conscience isn't a spade instead of a telescope, and would much rather do my best by my generation in a direct and practical way, than on the indirect and unpleasant principle of exposing my person to be kicked because it is exhilarating and healthy for my neighbour's toes.

'I think it would be a prouder and happier lot to be a simple unsophisticated Methodist preacher, with the power and the means to make a few souls better and happier, than to be the most advanced and acute speculator of the day.'

'But,' said I, 'what do you mean by saying you are prophecies of new opinions, early spring blossoms, etc., when you are always declaring that religions are and must be virtue-making machines, forcing or persuading men to improve ; and that your religion, not having the certainty, the dogmatism necessary to govern men's actions, cannot be of use to them ?'

'It is very difficult to imagine,' he replied, 'because it is always harder to look forward than back. We can easily imagine the barbarous times which preceded our present civilisation; it is almost impossible to conceive the extent to which it will be changed at the end of the next three thousand years. I do think and believe that my religion, or something like it, will have its day in course of time, in spite of its virtue-making deficiency for men as they are. It will come at last, like all other religions, by means of the strange law of inheritance of qualities and instincts. It seems to me that the succession of religions is like the succession of classes in a school. A child goes into the lowest class, and when he has learnt what that can teach him, he is moved into a higher one, and so on till he reaches the top. The same with religions. Man first enters into a low one; as soon as he has learnt what that can teach him, he is ready for a higher one (for the standard of the religion must always be above that of the mass who hold it to do any good), and he enters the higher one, the lessons he has learnt in the first not being obliterated and cast away, but so impressed on his mind as to require no further inculcation. And so on *ad infinitum*. And thus it is possible for me to imagine mankind gradually developed up to a point at which the moral laws, which he is now obliged to be cajoled and forced into by the leverage of a virtue-making machine, may, together with a powerful and ever-increasing moral sense, become so instinctive as to render the leverage of a virtue-making machine no longer necessary to maintain them.'

'There is a tremendous flaw in your speculation,' cried I; 'for you forget that, when men have reached a point at which our present moral law becomes instinctive (I am merely supposing your prophecy to be correct), they will require, according to your own theory, another and a higher virtue-making machine to drag them up to a still higher standard of good; the deficiencies of your religion as a virtue-making machine being therefore as fatal at that date as they are at this.'

'Very well put,' replied he. 'But I was imagining a period at which our moral sense should have developed to such a degree as to be creative and virtue-making in itself, thus doing away the necessity for the cajolement and terrorism in religion which are required during the childhood of mankind.'

'And how long,' asked I, rather sarcastically, 'will it take for this charming prophecy to fulfil itself?'

'How on earth should I tell?' replied he. 'Say ten thousand years, at a guess. The world is a slow-growing animal.'

'Well, there is no harm in your indulging in idle dreams, as long as you don't persuade yourself that you are going to see the fulfilment of them. But I don't see the good of them.'

'Don't you?' said he. 'All attempts to see

into the future must be dreams, and it is a short-sighted policy to forget the future and imagine that the world has been improved up to a certain point for our special benefit, and is going to remain there like a cart in a quagmire. So there is good in dreams, as there is in everything——'

'I have heard you make that remark before,' said I, drily.

'Allow me to give you a piece of advice,' answered he, oracularly, ' which is not cribbed either from a commonplace book or the pages of M. Tupper: "Never be ashamed to utter a truism, and don't break the sixth commandment when you hear one."'

CHAPTER V

'AND so my old man pitched into you, did he?' said I, amusedly, dangling my legs over the brink of the old wharf on which we were sitting.

'Yes,' replied he, half laughing, half vexed, 'it was the old story—"conceit." He quoted Dr. Liddon in answer to something I said, and I replied quite simply that I didn't agree, and was proceeding to say why, when he stopped me by a torrent of sarcasm. He began by declaring that he was quite sorry to think how grieved Dr. Liddon would be on hearing that I could not conscientiously endorse his opinions, and ended by telling me that I was a conceited young jackanapes, and that the sooner I was sent back to school and whipped whenever I opened my mouth without being asked a question the better. Conceit, indeed! He might as well call me conceited because I was born with brown hair while his was yellow, as call me conceited because my mind runs in a different groove from the one he thinks right.

I am quite tired of having to make the old defence that the man who——'

'Stop,' cried I. 'You don't seem to understand what it is makes people think you conceited. It is your cool disregard of all authority——'

'Which authority?' asked he, sharply.

'The authority,' continued I, 'of men far wiser, cleverer, and more learned than yourself. You disregard their conclusions as unhesitatingly as if they were mere tyros in the world of thought, and point out what you believe to be the roots of what you think their fallacies, as though you had the latch-key to all the greatest minds in the universe. It is no wonder that people think you conceited under these circumstances; and I tell you so the more openly, because I don't believe you are really very conceited at bottom.'

'Humph!' said he. 'Reminds me rather of a hanging scene I witnessed up in the islands, when the extempore hangman assured his victim as he swung him up, that if it was any comfort to him to hear it, he (the hangman) was convinced that he was entirely innocent. But to go to my defence: it is absurd to infer that because I avowedly disagree with Dr. Liddon, Sakya-Muni, Strauss, Mahomet, and a few millions more, that I therefore am conceited enough to think myself as clever, as wise, or as learned as any one of them. Such accusations of conceit spring from an utter misunderstanding of the nature of personal authority, which, carried to the extent that many people wish to carry it to, becomes a perfectly hopeless fallacy.'

'More conceit,' said I, smiling.

You be—be—gagged,' replied he. 'Can't you let a fellow show his mind honestly without crying "Yah, Peacock!" I thought you were above that sort of thing.'

'Never mind,' said I. 'Go on.'

'Well,' replied he, 'the principle of authority becomes a perfect sham if it is pressed beyond a certain point. Of course, though there is no physical reason preventing the tongue of an idiot from speaking truth, the opinions of a wise and clever man should be more closely examined, and more respectfully listened to, than those of more foolish and commonplace minds—that is to say, that the man *does* give importance to the opinion. So far so good. But an attempt to carry the principle of authority farther than this leads us into hopeless contradictions.'

'Expound,' said I.

'Have I not just said that the opinions of a wise and clever person are worth more than the opinions of a foolish and commonplace one—or words to that effect?'

'You have,' said I.

'Whence it follows that, supposing Jones, Brown, and Robinson, are three wise and clever men, and I in comparison a fool, I must accept the opinions of J. B. and R., and sink my own in favour of them.'

'Good,' said I.

'This,' continued he, 'is a bald sketch of the principle of authority. It would be sensible enough *if the wise men agreed.* But Jones, Brown, and Robinson, all clever, wise, and honourable men, contradict each other flat, so that I the fool (unless I am worthless enough to be content to put up my legs and think of nothing) am forced, not out of conceit, but out of sheer necessity, to criticise and pass judgment on the opinions of men that I know to be far cleverer and wiser than myself. Even if I cling wholly and blindly to one of them I make the principle of authority a mockery, for in following Jones I am disregarding the authority of Brown and Robinson. In point of fact, this principle, carried out impartially and strictly (which it seldom is), becomes the most blank, callous, indifferent form of scepticism that exists. It is odd that the religious people who are so fond of using one side of this weapon don't see that the back edge is cutting their own throats. Let us take a look into the roots of the question. I, a person of mediocre intellect, but in earnest, find myself in the world with the conflicting opinions of thousands of wiser and cleverer men than myself all round me. What am I to do? Cling blindly to the set nearest me, and swear they are the true ones till I am black in the face? I cannot do it. Decide which of the thousands of cleverer and wiser men than myself are on the right track? Surely that is an impossible feat for the wisest man in the world to perform.

How much more impossible to a person of mediocre intellect! Can I boil them all down together and take the essence? the materials won't mix. It seems to me that only two logical paths are open. Either to follow the principle of authority consistently to its goal of hopeless, purposeless scepticism, or else to try bravely, but humbly, to work out my own salvation—not judging the opinions of my superiors out of conceit, but simply because the fact that they disagree makes it necessary to every earnest man, great and small, to judge for himself—guessing at the roots of their opinions as nearly as I can from the working of my own mind,—never claiming Divine authority for my opinions, or infallibility for my conclusions—but being content to work honestly by whatever light God sees fit to send me. But what I wanted to impress upon your mind is, first, that as every man, whether consciously or unconsciously, does and *must* pass a judgment, either tacit or expressed, upon conflicting opinions, it is absurd to call any particular person conceited for so doing; and secondly, that the persons who talk loudest about authority are the people who regard it least.'

'Oh dear, you paradoxical young wretch, why?' groaned I. 'If you had been listening, instead of calculating how many eggs your hens are going to lay to-morrow morning, you would have heard,' retorted he. 'I showed that a perfectly impartial application of the principle of authority led necessarily to the boldest scepticism. Now, the people who talk loudest about authority are those who cling blindly to a scrap of it, and boldly deny that all the rest is authority at all. And having taken upon themselves to decide what particular men and opinions are to be taken as authorities to the exclusion of the rest, they laud themselves for their humility in following them, and upbraid their neighbour with conceit in his powers of judgment if he don't do likewise. What a farce it is! It's the same system as "Orthodoxy is my doxy, and heterodoxy your doxy;"—"Authority," say they, "is our authority, and yours isn't authority at all." I nearly caused your old man to assault me with violence on this question the other day. Having nothing particular to say in answer to one of my speeches, he tried the authority trick backed by an insinuation of conceit (a mode of combat that always makes me savage), and cried, "Surely, young man, you don't mean to say that you venture to set up your opinion against that of Butler?" etc. etc. "Surely, sir," retorted I, "you don't mean to say that you venture to set up your opinion against that of Strauss?" etc. etc. "Surely," cried he, angrily, "you don't mean to compare such men as Strauss, etc. etc. with such men as Butler?" etc. etc. "Surely, sir," snapped I, "you don't mean to compare such men as Butler, etc. etc. with such men as Strauss?" etc. etc.

'I was trying, by using his own mode of argument, to show him what an absurd will-o'-the-wisp the principle of authority comes to be when carried to such a length; but as he only called me an impertinent puppy, and went out of the room and slammed the door, I don't suppose I succeeded.'

'It *was* very impertinent of you,' said I, angrily, 'and it would have served you perfectly right if he had turned you out of the house, and refused to see you again.'

'I know it was very impertinent,' replied the boy very humbly, 'and I was very sorry afterwards, and went and begged his pardon, and he was very kind to me about it, but I am not altogether without an excuse. You know whenever I go up to your place in the evening, the dear old man puts his spectacles on his dear old nose, and rummages out Liddon's Sermon on Rationalism—charming sermons they are too— and sits himself bolt upright on his chair, and reads away till he comes to what he thinks a telling bit, which he delivers at me solemnly without note or comment, looking at me half triumphantly to see the effect, as if he had just heaved a cannonball into the middle of me. And I sit holding my tongue until I get so full of suppressed controversy that it bursts out, and then there's a row.'

'Why on earth can't you learn to hold your tongue?' said I. 'What possible satisfaction can there be in answering my old man about such things? O dear! I never knew the man yet who wouldn't be improved by being transformed into a woman for a month or two to teach him to be submissive for the sake of keeping the peace.

You are fond of making theories about the creation of woman; I believe she was invented as a kind of soothing syrup for male irritability.' I fancy I detected a slight twitching at the corners of Charlie's mouth—when he cried eagerly, 'Talking of women—listen!' I started, for, apparently close to us, a glorious fresh full voice rang out swellingly upon the still air, sounding against the sides of our hill-enclosed bay, as loud as if it had been in a room. Beautiful as the voice was, it was evidently untaught—and yet there was something in its want of art that suited admirably with the rude simplicity of the ballad.

'The sharp bow dashes swiftly round the headland clothed in spray,
 With slacken'd sheets the long white hull glides slowly up the bay,—
 Her hold is full of palm-oil, and sandal-wood, and gold,
 And her boats are fill'd with tropic fruit—as much as they will hold.

'And some one soon is telling me the story of the trip—
 How they met with Jack the pirate—how they gave the fiends the slip:
 Of a hurricane that caught them—of a passage they ran through—
 How they quarrell'd with some islanders, and lost a whole boat's crew.

'Ah! swiftly flew the moments when my love was by my side,
 In the days when he had vow'd to me that I should be his bride;
 But a gallant Southsea sailor ill likes a life of ease,
 And soon the sails were set once more to catch the southern breeze.

'Oh weary! oh, how weary, is my vigil on the shore,
Watching—weeping for a vision of a face I see no more:
For many a craft goes to and fro across the merry main,
But I am watching for a ship that never comes again.

'I dreamt that I was standing in a mist of colour'd spray,
On the steep edge of a coral reef two thousand miles away;
I peer'd down through the opal waves full thirty fathoms deep,
And there I saw a schooner's deck, and a sailor fast asleep.

'And I call'd him as he lay there, with his comrades round about,
He woke, and laugh'd the old laugh, "What love—hast found us out?
Our wedding-day is coming, love, for ere the year is past,
I shall fetch you to the haven where the sailors rest at last."

. . . . .

'To-morrow, sweet to-morrow, will end the weary year,
He is coming! He is coming! I feel him drawing near.
Death and he, like friends together, shall fly away with me,
To our home against the coral cliff beneath the tropic sea.'

'Where does the voice come from? who is it?' whispered I, as the last notes died away.

'The voice,' replied he, 'comes, if I am not mistaken, from behind that rock under the *Pohutikawa* on the water's edge, and the "Who" is Mary Stringer, Dan's daughter. Didn't you know that she had just come back from Auckland?'

'No,' replied I. 'What has she grown up like?'

'Oh, a regular devil to look at!' said he. 'I mean not pretty, but very handsome and mischievous-looking.'

'Oh!' said I. (The word 'Oh' is capable of great expression.)

My young gentleman declined to commit himself any further.

'I wish she would go on singing,' said he, lazily. 'The sound seemed to me to transform the whole bay. It was like a flood of light thrown suddenly upon a beautiful picture. It is a wonderful truth, that of Carlyle's, that the eye only sees that which it brings with it. I am very much obliged to you for being you, and sitting here. If you were a person I didn't like, you would entirely spoil my appreciation of the scenery.'

'Fiddlestick!' said I, caustically. 'That is because you have no real appreciation of a beautiful scene. Now *I* could enjoy this view for hours on end, with the most insufferable young prig in creation talking philosophy to me all the while.'

'That,' replied he, sleepily, 'is because your appreciation of a scene is so narrow—so merely technical, that it is not necessary to you that everything about you should be in harmony with it.'

I was about to say something crushing, when I was interrupted by the voice of my old man calling us in to dinner.

CHAPTER VI

Soon after the publication of the first chapter of 'Roots' the editor received the following letter :—

' "ROOTS."

'Dear Sir—Lo! the audacity of a poor remote little country mouse, who will officiously nibble the meshes which seem to have entrapped one great literary lion!

'The publication of "Roots" in your November number, has this month in its season propagated a species of bulb, which can only be a "root of bitterness."

'My dear sir, you know not what you do in admitting such to your pages; but since sanitary laws ought to be the more rigidly enforced upon and by those who are not alive to the risk of neglecting them, in the name of all that is sacred, confine the pages of *Temple Bar* to secular things, and let Religion and Irreligion fight their duel on another field. The safety-valve may swing upon a loose hinge, but all editorial weight should press upon the trap, which emits nothing but noxious vapour. Forget which is which; and as our mental and intellectual purveyor, you are answerable for furnishing diseased meat to our craving millions.

'True—the skipper of the "brave little cutter leaping furiously at the waves," may be a lovable private character—but if, in his contempt for *arrière pensée*, he will pitch overboard his quadrant (prayer), his compass (the Bible), his anchor (faith), his telescope (hope), his log-book (conscience), his ensigns (profession), and all the conventional paraphernalia which tend to make him a "machine-made" sailor, he is responsible for the lives, not only of all those who sail with him, but of all lookers-on who, trusting their lives to the security of their impulses, are content to toss themselves in exciting uncertainty on the billows of fancy.

'It was Wisdom who said, "It must needs be that offences come, but *woe* to him through whom they come."

'Would you ventilate *these* views, even though you may disown them?—and pardon, dear sir, the suggestions of

   'An obscure Well-wisher.'

This letter commands a certain amount of respect, for two reasons: in the first place, it expresses an opinion that would be felt equally by a large proportion of men of all countries in the world, of every religion that exists in it, on a mode of speculation such as is ventilated in 'Roots.' In the second place, it is not disfigured by the malignant dulness and reasonless assertion that usually accompany a justification of not thinking.

I must begin by saying, with all due deference to my anonymous friend, that the last part of his letter is hardly to the point, being a mere repetition (I hope he won't be shocked) of the whole spirit of the first chapter of 'Roots.' The one thing I tried to paint most conspicuously was my young friend's intense appreciation of the utility to mankind of the dogmas he thoroughly disbelieved in, and the impossibility at present of men's discarding them without harm. It seems a truism, at first sight, to say that a thing not perfect may do enormous good, even through its imperfections, but it is a truism not yet acknowledged as a truth in the world of religious thought. Who ever knew a missionary who thoroughly appreciated the good that was daily being wrought by the religion he was trying to supplant?

Now, my young friend's strongest characteristic was this power of liberal perception, springing from a firm belief in the omnipotence and omniscience of the unknown Creator, which taught him to look for a use and a purpose in everything.

The most enthusiastic priest could scarcely believe more firmly in the practical service performed by what the 'obscure well-wisher' calls, in metaphorical language, quadrants, compasses, anchors, telescopes, log-books, etc.; but he would say that their practical utility was quite apart from the question of their being perfect Divine truth.

His standpoint was something of this kind: 'I do not believe in the infallible Divine truth of either Christianity, Judaism, Mohammedanism, Buddhism, Hinduism, or Parseeism, or any other theory concerning unknowable things that now exists; I should not deem myself justified in claiming Divine authority for any creed, however beautiful, *having no prior knowledge of God to enable me to decide what His truth is;* but I can see the good all these contradictory religious beliefs have done and are doing; I can understand the good influence they supply and the voids they fill in men's minds; so I learn naturally to look on these as God's means to effect the improvement of humanity. When I call them "virtue-making machines" I am testifying to their worth. And when I see that the very quality I consider most wrong in them—*i.e.* their conceited assumption that they possess infallible truth, their utter ignoring of the great fact that religion is to an enormous extent an accident of birth—is the one that gives them their greatest power for good, I come to the simple conclusion that it is neither wise nor possible to improve them off the face of the earth. Of course they will die or change, as other religions have done before them, as soon as they become unsuitable and unnecessary to men's minds—but not before. I hold that a destruction of all these creeds from outside men's minds would do great harm. I say to my bugbear, "the conceited certainty of ignorance," or dogma, "I see the good you are doing. Go on in peace; but be not aggressive, for if your zeal takes the shape of persecution in any way I will knock you down, and laugh at you, and show the world what an unjustifiable sham you are. You will be put on the shelf and forgotten some day, but the time is not yet come. You are a pleasant wanton, and flatter men so delicately that they cannot bear to leave you, though conscience tells them it is time for their minds to go to work." I will go no further at present than to try, by showing the grounds on which scepticism stands, and differs from religious assertions, to clear away some of the barrowfuls of mud that are daily heaped upon it by ignorance and prejudice.'

This is a short sketch of his way of regarding all the religions of the world, watching the causes, uses, and effects of their different dogmas with an impartiality and a comprehensiveness that gave one the idea that he was taking a bird's-eye view of humanity with a telescope from a different planet—a way of judging that made him terribly alone among men; for even the small school that agreed with his criticisms on religious subjects could not as a rule keep their eyes open to the good that these condemned doctrines worked every day; they could not quite understand how he could demonstrate that some dogma was a groundless offspring of human conceit and want of faith, and yet believe, as strongly as any who held it, the work it did in the path of human improvement. He would say, 'Here is such and such a dogma—absurd, because it lays down the law positively on questions beyond human knowledge; and often leading to both blasphemy and cruelty when carried to the full length of its meaning; and yet it fills such a want in the human mind, and has such a strong practical power to influence men for good, that in spite of its absurdities and crimes it is better that men should believe in it as they are at present.' But the members of his little band of comrades, unconsciously imitating the narrow-mindedness of the fanatical priests they hated so bitterly, would reply in effect, 'It is untrue, therefore it must be destroyed. You yourself own that it leads to great evils, both of thought and action, and truth in any case must be acknowledged before utility.' And he would reply (Jesuitically, they used to say),

> 'Think not I'm one of those
> Who calmly claim omniscience, and suppose
> That God Almighty scarcely knows the worth
> Of this or that existing on the earth,
> And cry, "False creeds I cannot bear to see,
> Because I'm sure that God agrees with me."
> I feel but sure of one thing, which is this:
> *God's* truth is not quite what *I* think it is.'[1]

---

[1] This quotation has been introduced once before, but I think that a truth so generally forgotten—not only by the adherents of all

I myself thought him, not Jesuitical, but larger-minded than the rest of that little band of earnest thinkers that I loved so well (though he was by no means the cleverest), and appreciated the liberality which could utterly separate the question of the absolute truth of an opinion with its utility to that ever-changing, ever-growing phenomenon of nature—man.

The root, perhaps, of his freethinking lay in the fact that he simply could not judge of a corner of the world as if it was the whole—could not cut off a portion of the world's history and leave the rest half out of sight. The opinion so commonly held by men of *all* religions, that one portion of mankind have actually a patent for God's truth, while all the rest are groping about in a state of carnal darkness, was to him an absurdity rendered evident by the fact that men of *every* religion considered themselves the patentees; and he could not look on any stage of religious belief as utterly final, because of his firm conviction of the improvement of humanity.

He disagreed, he would laughingly say, with most of his sceptical comrades on a mere matter of dates. Both they and he were of opinion that a time would come when modes of thought would become far more unanimous, by all men pulling off (metaphorically speaking) the clothes of super-

religions, but also by their freethinking opponents—will stand a little repetition, and should be familiarised to men's minds by what my young friend would call the 'Poll-parrot system.'

stition and false claims to knowledge, and treading the earth with minds naked; but he differed from them by believing most firmly that the time for such a transformation had not come, that it would do harm—in fact, that an attempt to steal their mental breeches unawares would probably be impracticable, and if practicable, excessively mischievous.

Well, the way I laboured to demonstrate the two-sided phase of my young friend's mind on religious questions—the way I prosed to inculcate his belief in the superior power for good on men, as they are, of the lowest form of religion over the highest form of scepticism, in the plainest English, was simply piteous. The thought of the platitudes, repetitions, and simplifications on this subject that I had inflicted on the public quite sickened me for some days. But, lo! in the letter of an 'obscure well-wisher,' and all the comments, friendly and hostile, that I have heard on the subject, the moral and intent of the conversation have been entirely omitted. I begin to sympathise with the feelings of the unfortunate gentleman who cut his throat after trying vainly for an hour and a half to convince a deaf old lady that he thought it was a fine day. The fact is, that the general heterodoxy of the tone of thought stuck so fast in people's throats that they were unable to swallow any of the conclusions at all.

With regard to the first part of the letter, my

young friend would have said, 'Its spirit is that breathed in the glorious old nursery ballad—

'"'Tis the voice of the sluggard! I heard him complain,
You have waked me too soon, I must slumber again."

It is nothing, in fact, more than the usual defence of not thinking on such subjects.

'There is the usual cry of "Do confine your pages to secular subjects;" as if the commonest thing on the earth was not part of the same great mystery—as if religion should or could be something suspended in mid-air like a balloon; the usual implication that such questions are all comfortably settled, in defiance of the fact that all mankind are perpetually changing and differing about them; the usual not very flattering admission, that when such things are stirred up by the pole of honest investigation, they emit odours which require the compression of the religious nose; in short, the astounding assumption that this subject, which I venture to think by far the most important in life, is the only one on earth which is not to be honoured with the test of earnest impartial examination.

'The "let-it-alone" theory does not, in my opinion, treat religion with very real respect. The conclusions it leads to from its premises, that religious theories are not to be impartially and strictly examined, are something of this kind: "You are born into a world full of opposing religious theories. You are to lay hold of the one nearest to you and swallow it whole. Of course, if you chance to be born in England, you will be Christian; if in Turkey, Mohammedan; if in the Marquesas, Cannibal, and so on. You are not to examine into your creed with human reason or common sense, if Providence has given you any—that is sinful. You must shut your eyes to the fact that there are millions entirely disagreeing with your belief, and yet as positive that they are right as you are. *You may pass judgment on their convictions as much as you like.* You may call them names—you may pity them, if you feel inclined. Yes, you should pity them, certainly, because of their bad luck in not being born in the only country where the true faith exists. It was not the fault of that missionary that you eat the other day: it was only his bad luck in being born in the wrong part of the world, that prevented him from seeing the blessings of an enlightened cannibalism."

'Fancy some scientific man taking the non-investigation line about his theories. "So you want to know the grounds of my assertions, do you? I am right, and that is enough. Lots of people utterly disagree with me, do they? So much the worse for them, that's all I can say. Don't go bringing your 'diseased meat' of investigation here, sir. I am right, and—and—you! you are a conceited fool!"

'"But," the "obscure well-wisher" and many of his way of thinking will perhaps say, "the cases are not parallel; because we declare that religion is not a thing on which to exercise our human judgment." To which I reply, that in making such a declaration they were using their human judgment in a most unmistakable manner.

'The fact is, that you cannot entirely shift the responsibility of what you believe or disbelieve on to the shoulders of any church or creed. Whatever religious opinions you may hold, if you trace back the reasons why you believe them honestly to the end, you must find your human judgment and opinion at the bottom of them.

'The pious Romanist or Mohammedan who says, " I know such and such a doctrine is true, because it is in such and such a book ; and I know the book is true, because my religion says so ; *and I know (or am sure, or believe) that my religion is the true one,*" exercises his human judgment to a wider extent than the sceptic who says, " I do not think that my powers of judgment give me a right to lay down the law positively on matters upon which I see all the world disagreeing."

'It is an acknowledgment of this truth that turns men, generally bitterly against their inclinations, into sceptics ; so when religious folks revile them with " conceit " and a too great reliance on the powers of human judgment, they naturally return the accusation with interest—and so the pot and kettle call each other black.

'An acknowledgment of this fact, that the root (however far back it may lie) of what a man believes or disbelieves is grounded on personal judgment and opinion, would go far to produce the toleration that I and many others desire to see; but I do not suppose that religions will open their eyes to it if they can help it, for it would place the opinions they worship on a lower, though a truer pedestal.'

Now these are the sort of comments that my young friend would probably have made on the letter of the 'obscure well-wisher.' I myself am unable to see all the method of thought that he supposes is implied in it. It seems to me that all the 'obscure well-wisher' meant by his rather abusive language was, that such kind of writing is noxious (whether true or false), because it may do harm to some minds by weakening the strength of the religion that has hitherto had power to keep them virtuous—a question that my young friend (as I have shown) regarded as nearly an open one, in his cool moments. What was the final conclusion that he came to, on the probable balance of the good *versus* the evil likely to be produced by the non-concealment of free thought, will be related in the next and last chapter of 'Roots.'

Yet I do not think that I have erred in putting these not strictly pertinent comments into his mouth, for he knew, poor fellow! from bitter experience, the kind of religious thought which called free honest thought by such names as 'diseased meat' and 'noxious vapours,' and would at once suspect it, whether it lay behind these expressions or not, and, in his indignant vindication of his own style of thinking, would forget his usual impartiality for the moment. He did not possess a perfect temper, poor boy! Under his peculiar mental circumstances it would have been strange if he did.

Let us get out of this bitter atmosphere for a while, and refresh ourselves with a sniff of the sea-breeze.

Our little bay is looking brighter, greener, wilder than ever. The white flashes on the open water in the distance promise a quick passage to Auckland for the little cutter that lies twenty yards from the shore getting ready for sea. Dan Stringer, a fine young half-caste without a surname, called Jack, and my young friend, are loading her, by means of a dingey and a punt, with firewood; while the sailors, with equal speed and energy, stow the cargo as fast as it comes on board. On a rock close to them sits Dan's half-caste daughter Mary, about to return to the custody of friends in town, for whom, in spite of my selfish delight at getting rid of her, I cannot help feeling a sincere pity. For she had already begun to sow discord in our little paradise. Jack already has fallen desperately in love with her, and wears a Cain-like expression of face whenever she speaks to any one but himself; while she, though too thorough a flirt to discard his attentions entirely, cares for him a little less than her father's kangaroo dog. One glance, as she sits there, at the tall womanly figure and the dark, dare-devil, irregular beauty of her face, directing (as I fancy) occasional flashes of fascinating softness towards my young friend, would convince the most superficial observer that she ought not to be allowed to go anywhere without being decorated with a warning red flag.

Dr. Watts once made a proverb about idleness, with which all my readers are doubtless familiar. It was exemplified in this case by my young friend taking it into his head that it was his business—the young prig—to devote himself to this young lady's education. Now, the process of a young gentleman of twenty-one educating a young lady of eighteen is, in my opinion, not unlike that of warming a heap of loose gunpowder with a lighted match.

Educationally speaking, the experiment was a decided success. She, ordinarily utterly wild and intractable, proved a most willing and obedient pupil. She would pore over the same book with him for hour after hour without showing a sign of weariness; she would go long walks with him, and listen to, and remember, and believe every word that he spoke; in short, he taught her more in a week than she had learnt in four years of school; but still I had very strong misgivings, which every mother of a family will understand, as to whether the end, taken as a whole, would quite justify all these proceedings.

It strikes me as something ghastly that I should be able already to write so lightly of all this. Well! well! Time and a busy life combined will soon blunt the most painful remembrance ; but if I could only have guessed —— stop : I am getting on too fast. Let us enjoy our little glimpse of sunshine before the black clouds murder it.

With my hat dangling from my fingers, I stroll lazily towards the rock where 'the firebrand' is sitting. Ordinarily reserved and silent, in spite of her wild mischief, she is more so than ever now, and answers all my platitudes with mechanical monosyllables, whilst the tearless black eyes have a look about them that I have never seen before. 'Humph!' think I to myself with an indignant sniff; 'here's a pretty mess that reckless young gentleman has been making in his character of male schoolmistress! Thank goodness the silly girl is going out of the place.' Women, even while making common cause against their common enemy, men, contrive to think very cruelly of each other.

Meanwhile, our conversation having died a natural death, I stroll nearer to where the work is going on. There is a general atmosphere of energy, perspiration, and, it must be owned, occasional forcible language. The little punt, with timber piled high above her gunwale, is shoved off for the last time, Jack the half-caste standing on top of the heap, and paddling cautiously towards the cutter. He inclines his weight in the least degree to one side, and the overladen little craft turns slowly and solemnly over, spilling Jack and all his cargo into six feet of water ; whereon, both from his unsanctified lips and those of Dan, came a chorus of exclamations so horribly expressive that I was forced to stop my ears for very shame.

'I shouldn't think you found this society altogether improving,' cried I, indignantly, to my young friend, who was standing close to me at the moment.

'It's not pleasant language to listen to, certainly,' replied he with a cool grin, 'but it is only language—neither more nor less than their way of expressing "What a bore." Dan and Jack are good men and true; shall I discard them because they speak a foreign tongue?'

'You are incorrigible in the matter of excuses,' cried I, marching with scornful dignity out of earshot, while he went back to help to collect the floating timber.

At last the work was finished and the cutter ready for sea. My young friend (rather unnecessarily, I thought) carried Mary into the dingey and sculled her on board, at which poor Jack looked as black as thunder. The dingey came back, the anchor was weighed, the sails loosed, and amidst a multitude of good-byes, and a parting chorus of chaff between Dan and the sailors, the little vessel rounded Farewell Point and was lost to view; and, as the end of the main-boom disappeared behind the rocky cliff, I found myself unconsciously heaving a sigh of relief. With a civil 'God day' Dan shouldered his axe and trudged stoutly homeward, like one who had done his duty as a woodcutter and a father, while poor Jack sauntered off with a listless air that told pretty plainly what he was thinking of. My young friend laid himself out to dry in the sun, as if colds and rheumatism were as yet uninvented.

'I'm glad she's gone,' said I, significantly, nodding seawards.

'Poor little black cat, why?' inquired he, with dutiful unconsciousness.

'Can't you, or *won't* you, see that you were making poor Jack more crazy with jealousy every day?' asked I, sharply.

'The sooner poor Jack gets accustomed to that the better,' answered he, rather pityingly, 'for, if I don't make him jealous you may be sure half a dozen other people will. Why, I believe that girl did flirt with her godfather when she was in long clothes, and will flirt with the clergyman who administers to her the last consolations of religion.'

'Well,' said I, forcibly, 'if she comes down here again she will bring mischief with her.'

'That's as certain as the sunrise,' replied he, with a lazy laugh. And here I stopped short. If I could only have foreseen, but it is too late to think of that now. The fact was, that, honourable and trustworthy as I knew my young friend to be, I could not hide from myself that to tell him that I knew the girl loved him already would be to break one of the most decided and sacred laws of that very contradictory and elastic catalogue— the feminine code of honour. 'She won't marry

Jack,' added he, after a pause, during which he had been reflecting, taking shots at a bit of wood floating in the water; 'and if she did she would make his life miserable by her vanity and wilfulness. What a strange mixture of comedy and tragedy some women are! They will break their hearts and their necks too to get the rubbishing apple that hangs out of their reach, and kick aside contemptuously the far finer one that lies at their feet.'

'Don't be priggish,' interrupted I. 'I am no admirer of the shallow claptrap of young cynics. Their half-true platitudes are made neither wise nor witty by being feebly malicious.'

'I really think,' continued he, smiling and taking no notice of my caustic admonitions, 'that the Persian legend of the creation of woman must be the right one after all. Would you like to hear it?'

'I can see by your face,' said I, resignedly, 'that it is something impudent and silly, but as time and experience only can teach you greater wisdom and humility, you may as well go on.' He took no more notice of me than if he had been deaf. The fact was, that I was a great deal too fond of the boy to snub him properly, and like most spoilt children, he was quite aware of the fact.

'To begin with,' said he, 'I have several reasons for believing that the story of the Garden of Eden was taken, during the Babylonish captivity, with many other things, from the Magians, and adopted by the Jews. By the way, what an interesting study it would be to trace the influence of their grand old monotheism[1] (for it was originally a real Monotheism, until that stumbling-block, "the origin of evil," tripped them up, like all the rest of the world) on Judaism, and through that on Christianity and Mohammedanism!'

'Oh, that theology!' cried I, despairingly; 'whatever we talk about seems to lead back to that eternal subject.'

'So it should,' replied he, rebelliously. 'As all theology takes its root in man's impressions and theories on all that he sees around him, it is more or less indissolubly connected with everything, and——'

Here I stopped my ears, and he, consequently, his tongue.

'Let us to the legend, then,' said he. 'Whether it is one held to be absolutely authentic by the modern Parsees, who are the sole remnant of the once widespread faith, I know not, but it differs from the Jewish one in one very important particular, as you shall hear.

'Ormuzd (the Good Deity) had placed Adam in the Garden of Eden, giving him full power and

---

[1] The deity of Zoroaster was too far off, too intangible, to suit or have hold on the minds of men, so his disciples, like all the rest of the world, dragged him down to the level of their comprehension, by making him a perfect idealised man-spirit, and invented a devil, to account for pain and evil. And so this Monotheism died out of the world, as all *real* ones have as yet done.

authority over everything in it, except the tree of knowledge and the tree of life. But after a while he thought that it was not good for man to be alone, and he determined to create woman. So he threw Adam into a deep trance under a tree in the garden, and took a rib from his side, wherewith to make woman. And Ormuzd stood there, turning the rib over in his hands, like one not quite sure of the wisdom of what he was doing; and the more he thought about it the more he determined to take time to consider. So at last, he laid the rib down by Adam's side, and calling an angel to come and watch it, went for a walk in the garden. Now whether this angel was tired from flying on errands or from fighting the followers of Ahriman, or whether the weather was hot and drowsy, the legend saith not; it merely states that the angel went fast asleep at his post.

'Now, as luck would have it, the great Father of Apes came sauntering by, brimful of curiosity, as usual; and he examined Adam, and he examined the angel, and finally he examined the rib, till at last, having fully satisfied himself that it couldn't possibly belong to him or be any business of his, or be of any possible use to him, he determined (this is monkey-reasoning) to appropriate it. This done, he proceeded to climb the tree under which the sleepers were lying, to have a more deliberate examination of his newly-acquired treasure. But in so doing, he knocked a bit of bark on to the angel's nose; this woke him, and seeing the rib gone and the monkey above his head, he realised what had happened, and flew up the tree in pursuit. But the monkey gained the topmost boughs, while the angel's wings became entangled in the branches, so that the most he could do was to seize the end of the monkey's tail and pull lustily. But the monkey held on like grim death, and refused to drop the bone, while, to the angel's horror, he heard Ormuzd walking slowly towards the tree. He gave one desperate tug, and away he went crashing to the bottom of the tree, with the monkey's tail in his hands. With great presence of mind, he laid the tail down by Adam's side exactly where the rib had been. Absently and pensively Ormuzd walked up, and without further scrutiny transformed the tail into a woman.

'This exquisite legend accounts for several things. In the first place it tells us how apes came to have no tails. Secondly, it gives us the key to Eve's fatal curiosity. Thirdly, it explains why women are—ahem!—women.'

'It amuses me,' remarked I, scornfully, 'to watch you playing at being a misogynist, or a "gynothrope," as Mayne Reid delightfully calls it in one of his books. I have always noticed that small-minded men, who are peculiarly enslaved by admiration and respect for women, take a mean bombastic delight in proclaiming their contempt for them as loudly as possible.'

'Be pacified,' cried he, laughing. 'Has not the

great Darwin shown that very likely men, as well as women, are descended from the same hairy parent? And upon my word,' added he, 'a study of the *jeunesse dorée* of the present day has almost led me to believe he is right.' After a pause he continued—

'The "prodigal son" of the nineteenth century is a strange animal truly. Like an animal, he is negatively bad more than positively. His only business is the pleasure of the moment. He is scarcely wicked, because his moral nature is so blunted that he really never thinks what is wrong and what right, except in the matter of violating some "honour among thieves" kind of law which he and those like him have made sacred. His soul is drugged till it is well-nigh dead. He is generally a simple believer in the religion he has been brought up in, because thinking is not in his line; but as for realising his religion and trying to act up to it, that is not in his line either. He is *the* most exasperating specimen of humanity to all earnest people of whatever opinions, excepting his brother, "the respectable worldling"—a type to be met in all nations and classes. His law (by no means a bad one, mark you) is that of conventional respectability. The religious faculties of his mind are quite as fast asleep as those of his sinful brother, and he looks on all who are not as stupefied as himself as more or less crazy. If you told him he was an infidel, he would be honestly astonished and indignant. Yet, as far as not realising and not caring about what he professes to believe, he is an infidel to the backbone. Like Gallio, he cares for none of these things. He may be an amiable worldling or an unamiable one, but a godless animal worldling he is, not only not seeking, but not feeling the want of, mental inquiry and realisation in religion.

'These two brothers, so unlike in their outward life, so like as regards thought and religion, are, as I said, the most intolerable bugbears to earnest men of all sorts. The preacher thunders at them from the pulpit; the freethinker shoots bitter words at them from his study; but still, smiling like South Sea Islanders under the influence of *kava*, the worthless, selfish, profligate, godless prodigal, and his equally godless, thoughtless, respectable brother, float calmly down the river of life, continually run into by the barks of their living-souled fellow-creatures, yet, like the elastic surf-boats of Madras, never the least feeling the effects of a collision.

'Well, believing as I do that everything in the world has a purpose, whether we can see it or not, I cannot call them unmitigated evils. I fancy, moreover, that I can see the good worked by that sluggishness and shallowness of mind that priests and sceptics alike detest so bitterly. For they act as a drag and a safeguard upon humanity, doing good to their kind by sheer indifference. Suppose all these people cleared out of the world, and the earnest people left to themselves. The whole lot of them would be carrying out their opinions to their logical or illogical consequences, till, either metaphorically or literally, they hung each other in every market-place. Whereas as things are now, when a tendency of such a kind is displayed, these great, lazy, apparently worthless giants rouse themselves yawningly, saying, with a kind of sluggish common-sense: "Now listen. I don't know which of you people are right and which wrong, and what's more, I don't care. But this kind of row isn't the right thing, and I want to sleep comfortably; so, if you are not quiet, I'll gag the lot of you."

'And this animal indifference of theirs does good too in a nearly opposite direction; for it stimulates earnestness even while it checks its possible consequences. A great vice produces almost invariably an opposing virtue. The impurity of a nation produces a Puritan reaction, and so on.'

'So,' said I, sarcastically, 'let us inscribe on the tombstone of every horrible criminal:

' " Stranger ! here lies one
Who
(Whether you be Saint or Sinner)
Has done as much as you
In his own peculiar Fashion
Towards the Improvement of Humanity." '

'And how do you know,' replied he, 'that the life and example of every criminal do not teach a good lesson to humanity ? The ascetic purity of early Christianity was greatly aided by the filthy licentiousness around it. Great drunkenness and its consequences produce a fanatical Temperance party. In fact, the presence of sin stimulates virtue.'

'When I was a little girl they used to teach me that evil communications corrupted good manners,' said I.

'I never denied,' cried he, impatiently, 'that what we call sin spreads sin, but merely stated that at the same time it stimulates virtue. When a man comes in contact with some crime, one of two things usually happens: either he is seduced by it, or he is horrified by it, his love of virtue being thereby stimulated. Why, it is a mere truism to say that men are deterred from sin by seeing its consequences.'

'Well,' retorted I, provokingly, misunderstanding his drift, 'it is a comfort to think that it is so easy to improve the world that one can do it by sinning comfortably. Why don't you give us the benefit of your help by committing a murder or two?'

But he heeded me not, for, rising to his feet, and gazing wildly over the crisp blue sea at the many-coloured hills beyond, he was following the path of his thoughts:—

'In all that glorious landscape there is not one particle of matter, animate or inanimate, that is not apparently at war with another, destroying or being destroyed—that is not really changing or being changed. Death is creating life and life death at every moment, in every place; for though apparently employed in mutual annihilation, their strife is but the striking of an awful but harmonious chord. What seems destruction is but fresh creation. So too with good and evil—Ormuzd and Ahriman.

'Their seemingly destructive antagonism is the key to their ceaseless existence. Every deadly blow that they strike generates fresh force. Can it be that ever Ormuzd should utterly conquer Ahriman, and bring the promised Millennium? We cannot imagine it, for Evil being utterly destroyed, Good would become a nonentity, and life would not be life, or the world the world. Yet we know not. Somewhere adown the dim vista of eternity it *may* come to pass that the two powers, wrestling closer and closer in their creative struggle, may at last become one, and thus pass into non-existence, the life of each having been dependent on that of the other. But we cannot imagine it. For to render it possible, change and antagonism in the world, which seem now to be the mainspring of its existence, must have ceased. We cannot conceive it paralysed at the halting-point of perfection. And while change through antagonism is the mainspring of its existence, what we call pain and misery must in some form or other remain. *Our* path seems to be plain: to trust the purpose of it all blindly to the Almighty Power, and to suffer and be brave.'

And as he stood there with his hair fluttering in the breeze, and a rigid, painful earnestness expressed in his attitude, his hands, his eyes, and every line of his face, a sense of awe stole over me, for it seemed for the moment as though I were looking upon the embodied type of all the truth-loving, sorrowing men that have existed through all ages, who have been driven almost to madness by a knowledge of their ignorance, by a sense of the insoluble mystery of everything around them.

I broke the spell, saying quietly, 'There is "death in the pot." The only hope you hold out as legitimate is so utterly vague that the moral of all you have said seems plainly to be, "Let us eat and drink, for to-morrow we die."'

'To me,' replied he, 'the moral seems to be, "Let us strive to develop in ourselves a complete trust in God, a great unselfish love for our fellow-creatures, and a manly courage, until the very miseries of our life seem to us means of improvement."'

I shook my head. 'A very ingenious and almost miraculously orthodox conclusion for your wild speculations to lead to; but it seems to me that if mankind were persuaded that the drones and criminals were as necessary to the improvement of mankind as the earnest and virtuous, they would tend towards idleness and crime themselves, crying, " *Sessa!* Let the world slide."'

My young friend paused awhile, and I flattered

myself that he was posed; but after performing a *post-mortem* examination on a dead crab he replied, 'I am not quite sure of that. I said that the drones and the criminals were as necessary as the earnest and virtuous in the work; first, because they act as a drag upon the extremes which earnest people are always apt to run into; and secondly, because, by the law of repulsion and antagonism which I afterwards wandered away upon, they irritated and strengthened earnestness and virtue. I don't think that an acknowledgment of this fact need make a man either a drone or a criminal.

'Take an analogy in politics. We will suppose a man to be a conscientious Liberal. Yet, unless he is a mere fanatic, he will own that an opposition on the whole is a good thing, because it is a safeguard against over-hasty legislation, checking sudden and often faulty impulses and principles. To carry out the analogy, he would very likely own, further, that by the very fact of its being an opposition it did good in another way, by sharpening the wits and the energy of the side he believed right. He does not become any the less a conscientious and earnest Liberal because he owns this fact.'

I really don't know how to answer this, so take refuge in satire. 'It seems to me,' said I, 'that your theory of the use of evil is much like the Spanish one of the use of beggars. When a Spaniard sees a beggar, which he does every ten yards he walks, he gives him a small coin, with the philosophical reflection that it is a great mercy that beggars exist, because if they didn't neither he nor any one else would have the means of getting to Heaven.'

'It seems to me,' replied this impudent young person, mimicking my voice and manner, 'that your method of dealing with a point under discussion is much like a sight I once saw of a poor half-paralysed wretch trying to eat his dinner. He made so many bad shots at his mouth with his fork that he finally gave it up in despair, and left off hungry. Let us get up on Farewell Point and see if the cutter is still in sight.'

And we clambered up, and lay down in the long grass to regain our breath. The breeze had died away, and the little cutter, not two miles off, was rocking lazily on the swell.

However unartistic it may seem, I must honestly confess that this slight circumstance did not fill me with any vague mysterious presentiments. Nor do I, like some people I have met, have my presentiments *afterwards*. But as my eyes wandered lazily from the little cutter to the thoughtful face of my young friend, I rejoiced secretly over the departure of the 'firebrand,' and wondered vaguely what would happen if she came back again.

'What are you thinking about?' asked I, suddenly and sharply.

'I was thinking,' replied he, scrutinising my face with a mischievous twinkle in his eyes, 'how dreadfully sea-sick that unfortunate girl must be at this moment. And what, pray, were *you* thinking of?'

'I was thinking,' said I, 'that—that you looked as if you thoroughly believed in your pet proverb: "Idleness with contentment is great gain."'

CHAPTER VII

SIX months had passed away since the departure of Mary Stringer for Auckland, when, on a fine spring morning, I was startled from my work by the hoarse rattle of a chain in the landlocked harbour; and, running down to the shore, found myself close to the vessel that had just anchored, and on her deck saw, to my intense dismay, the young lady in question.

Beautiful, dangerous, reserved and cat-like as ever, she received all our greetings with the calmest self-possession, shook hands with my young friend as though he was the nearest acquaintance—an incident that, for some reason that I can't quite define, gave me a shiver of dread—asked if there was any chance of her father coming down the bay that afternoon, and if not, whether any one would be kind enough to row her and her luggage up to the head. Jack was there, and would be delighted, of course—Poor Jack!

The time that followed—the terrible catastrophe it ended in—I cannot yet dwell upon without almost unbearable pain, and so I shall describe what took place as shortly and as simply as I can.

Three days had not passed before Mary and my young friend had slipped back into their former positions of tutor and pupil, while Jack became a more infatuated and more hopeless worshipper than ever. A child might have foreseen that such a state of things would bring mischief and sorrow to some one of the three, and I made up my mind at last to interfere.

I first tried to do something, through Dan, and was completely unsuccessful. In the first place, he looked on my young friend as the king who could do no wrong. Secondly, he, not without reason, declared that his daughter was so strong-willed and so reserved, that an attempt on his part to remonstrate against anything she chose to do would be utterly futile. 'As for Jack,' said he, 'I've got no patience with such as he. If the girl will have him, let him take her; if she won't, let him make his mind up to it like a man, instead of going tearin' and bellowin' an' moanin' about like a wild cow that's lost her calf. I do deride at such stuff.'

And then I tried Mary herself, and found that Dan knew his daughter's character better than I expected. She was extremely civil, with the faintest dash of sarcasm in her civility. She utterly refused to be drawn into a discussion upon the subject — thanked me very coldly for the interest I had shown in her welfare; in fact, somehow managed to put me in the wrong, and to make me leave her baffled, humiliated, and angry, both with myself and every one else.

And then I did what I ought to have done at first: I spoke to my young friend without reservation. He exasperated me at first more than the others had done. 'What a to-do about nothing!' cried he, laughing. ' Why, so far from there being any too great tenderness between us, I have laughed at her innate tendency to flirtation till she scarcely dares say good morning to me with decent civility for fear of my tongue!'

Oh, the blind idiocy of the male mind! Here was the whole mischief laid bare to my feminine one in one sentence. If he had been the most accomplished *roué* in the world, he could not have adopted a surer plan to break the vanity and win the heart of a vain, wilful, passionate, half-educated girl like Mary.

'You silly boy,' said I, impatiently, ' what do you suppose it is that makes her receive your scoldings humbly, while she will fly out at the most gentle reproof from any one else? What is it that makes her prefer your rudeness to any one else's flattery?'

'Love of variety, I suppose,' said he, doubtingly, and then held his tongue to think. After a while he continued, 'I begin to see many little things in a new light, and believe you are right. What shall I do?'

'Do!' cried I, energetically. 'Get away from the island at once, and don't come back until I can get the girl sent back to her relations in town again;'—and I made a mental resolve that on this occasion Miss Mary should find me as obstinate as herself. 'My husband is thinking of going to Taupo, to look at a run that is offered for sale. You shall get instructions from him and go instead. When will the cutter sail?'

'She ought to have all her cargo on board by noon to-morrow,' replied he, 'and I will go in her. I do believe you're the best-hearted old woman that ever lived!'—and I ran into the house delighted, to mature my scheme.

To-morrow! To-morrow! I was one day too late.

The events that occurred before nightfall I will relate as they were told me by the actors concerned.

On the very morning that this conversation with my young friend took place Jack had gone up to Dan's hut, and pleaded his love to Mary, for the third time. She, poor girl, was herself in a fretful, anxious state of mind, and he irritated her into dismissing him rudely—almost insultingly. All the wild beast in his uneducated nature was roused. He turned as he left her, and whispered hoarsely, 'I know who's the cause of this, curse him! and if I don't pay him for it'—I can't repeat the rest of the sentence.

'You had better not,' replied the girl, contemptuously, 'if you care for your own life;' and poor Jack blundered out heedlessly into the bush, giddy and sick with rage. For some time he wandered about through the forest, trying to think, but one thought kept possession of his mind: 'The infernal scoundrel! he has broken her heart and mine too. not because he cares a d—— for her, but just for amusement. Curse him! I'll pay him for it!' and then he directed his steps steadily in the direction of our bay. Straight over the hills and across the gullies he held his way, heedless of the chattering birds overhead, heedless of the wild pig he startled from its lair, heedless of the little fish that darted wildly up and down the little creeks as he splashed through them, heedless of everything but his determination to find the man who had injured him, and to say and do—he knew not what.

Meanwhile my young friend, as soon as our conversation was over, had shouldered a sack, a pick, and a spade, and had marched off to a place about half a mile up the harbour, where he had discovered a splendid mine of *kauri-gum*, with the intention of digging up as much of it as he could, and taking it up with him to Auckland for sale, intending thereby to realise a couple of sovereigns; and having discovered the stick by which he had marked the spot, he worked away till he had got as much as the sack would hold, and strolled to the edge of the cliff hard by, where he sat down to smoke his pipe and rest his aching back. It was a favourite spot of his—a network of branches overhead, another below his feet growing out of the face of the cliff. Peering through the latter you could see the still water about thirty feet below, and in it generally a gigantic stingaree, lazily coasting around the black rocks. And as he lay there in peaceful solitude he subjected himself to a severe cross-examination about his behaviour to Mary. The more he examined it the worse he found it. He had been culpably thoughtless and thoughtlessly selfish. What possible right could he have had to dissect her mind as he would the body of a dead rat? What business was it of his to try and work her intellect up to a higher level than that of the people she belonged to? Had he done it from a good motive? Well, he had, partly. He had seen that unless her energies were directed to higher things they would devote themselves to low ones—that without education she promised fair to become a thoroughly mischievous, dangerous woman, but his chief reason for doing it had been the interest and amusement the task brought him. He came to the conclusion that he had been a vain, meddlesome, selfish, thoughtless fool.

But I would beg those who read this, however much inclined they may be to agree with the poor boy's comments on his own conduct, not to judge him too hardly. Let them ask themselves how many young men they know who could withstand the subtle flattery conveyed in a fascinating, wilful girl being soft to them and them only, obedient to their will and to none other. How many they know honourable enough never to use their influence for the slightest mischievous purpose?—honourable enough to cast that influence away without hesitation the moment they found the secret of its spell—above all, honourable and simple enough to be ashamed of having gained such influence, instead of triumphing in their power? Cast loose upon the world at the age of sixteen by an enraged Tractarian father, it is not to be wondered at that his life had been a wild and venturous though never a vicious one; and as he lay in the long grass and turned over his late conduct in his mind, he could not help being half amused at the serious way in which he was regarding what a year or so ago he would have called an unfortunate accident. He supposed that the pure solitude of his life had restored the sensitive innocence of his nursery days. Perhaps it had. Should he marry her? The fact of her being the daughter of a runaway sailor and a savage did not make much odds in the land he had resolved to stay in. But could he love her? Yes! in a kind of way he did already, but not as a young man should love the woman he marries. He loved her as he loved his pet dog; he could not look on her as a being to be respectfully and ecstatically worshipped. If he were ten years older, and had a little more romance kicked out of him, it might do, but now—the best thing he could do for all parties was to vanish.

And as he came to this wise conclusion he heard the breaking of a stick, and turning himself on his elbow, found himself face to face with Jack. The two kept silence; Jack glaring at his foe with a kind of stony fury, the other noting the expression of his face with an honest pang of shame and remorse. There was no sound but the measured panting of Jack's lungs. Hop! pit! pat! A fearless little bird settled on the ground between them, picked up the fragment of a twig, and darted away; in the branches overhead a judicial-looking *caw-caw* established himself comfortably to watch the proceedings. At last Jack cast his eyes down sullenly, and spoke:

'Master Charles, I've got an account to settle with you.'

'Well, out with it,' was the reply.

Jack's lips moved painfully and noiselessly for a few seconds: then thickly and slowly came, 'Do you intend marryin' Mary Stringer?' and he held his breath, waiting for the reply.

'It's not your business, Jack; but I'll answer your question. No.'

'Then,' burst out the poor fellow, 'you are an infernal scoundrel, and I'll thrash you within an inch of your —— life. Get on to your feet, you coward!'

My young friend never stirred.

'Calling me a coward,' he said quietly, 'is nonsense. You don't believe it yourself. We've got all the afternoon to fight in, if fight we must; for the present, just listen to me. You know I never tell lies; and I declare to you on my honour that I have never intentionally tried to stand between you and Mary, and have never in *any* way made love to her in my life.'

It was a curious proof of the respect in which he was held, that Jack, though naturally incapable of understanding the kind of friendship his rival felt towards the girl, though perfectly mad with fury, believed what he said unhesitatingly.

'Oh no!' cried he, distorting his features into a hideous sneer; 'you wouldn't go to make love to her. You wouldn't bemean yourself by doing nothin' so low and debasin' as that. But its high old fun for you to go and turn the girl's head by filling it with a lot of rubbish, till she looks on all her old friends as the dirt beneath her feet. If the girl's fool enough to fall in love with you, that's her fault, in course; and if a poor devil like me breaks his heart about it, that's another unfortinit accident. You ain't done nothin' wrong in your little amusement!' And Jack laughed a short convulsive laugh, terrible to hear.

There was a leaven of truth in his sneer that went home to my young friend's heart, and he resolved to make another attempt at pacification.

'Look here, Jack. If what you have said is true, I am very sorry. I am going to leave the island to-morrow, and shan't come back till Mary is gone or married.'

'So you mean sneakin' off now, do you?'

retorted Jack. 'I'm d——d if you leave the island, or this spot either, before I've left my marks on you. Get up and fight, curse you! or I'll kick you up.'

'All right,' replied my young friend, getting up and preparing to fight with that peculiar absence of anything like malice so characteristic of Englishmen; 'I'm ready.'

As far as strength and weight went, there was not much to choose between them, but in temper and skill they were no match at all. Jack pushed in desperately to fight at close quarters, but he never had the slightest chance. At last, half stunned with blows that might have killed a weaker man, he charged furiously at his antagonist, who quietly waited for him, sprang lightly on one side, and putting his foot on a loose stone as he hit out, lost his balance, and crashing through the branches, fell with a dull thud on the rocks below.

For an instant Jack stood thunderstruck. And in that instant all the wrath and jealousy died out of his heart, and he thought of the man with the respect and love of the old days, before Mary came back from school. He peered down through the bushes, and saw the body lying motionless, half in, half out the water.

'Master Charles!' said he, hardly daring somehow to speak above his breath.

'It's no use your scrambling down here, Jack,' answered a quiet voice. 'Go round to the house bay and get a boat. Quick! for the tide's rising and I can't move.'

There was no need to hurry poor Jack. In half an hour he had brought him home, and was running to our house for help. I sought the poor boy's cottage at once, with what anxiety and grief I need not say. No doctor could be fetched for two or three days; but it needed no doctor to tell us that the case was hopeless, for his back was broken. All he told us was that he had put his foot on a loose stone, and fallen down the cliff; but Jack, in his sorrow and remorse, blurted out the true story at once. At last he said—

'If somebody must go for a doctor it had better be Jack. He can take the small lifeboat, and sail at once. Yes, you must go, Jack, or there will be mischief between you and Dan. Don't blame yourself about this unlucky business, old fellow; it was all an accident, and I hope you forgive me for the trouble I have brought you. Good-bye.'

And Jack took the proffered hand, and staring blankly at the smiling face, said, 'I wish I was dead!' and walked quietly out of the room.

Dan and Mary, as soon as they heard of what had occurred, took up their quarters at his cottage, and two kinder, gentler nurses the poor boy could not have had.

In three days the doctor arrived—'the first of the vultures,' as poor Charlie remarked, with one of his old quaint *moues*. They had a long talk together; and, going into the room, I found, to my astonishment, the doctor doubled up with laughter in a chair by the bedside. On leaving it with me, his face saddened suddenly.

'What a pity! what a pity!' said the good old man, with real feeling. 'One of the finest and pleasantest young fellows, both in mind or body, I ever met! How long will he live, madam? Upon my word, I can't tell you exactly; he may linger on for days, weeks, or perhaps even months. I wish I could do anything for him; but he has done with this world, poor boy.'

And I grieved silently and bitterly, for I loved him as my own son. He had fallen amongst us homeless, friendless, and lonely; and it is little wonder that all of us, but I more than all, learnt to love a character so gentle, so earnest, so clever, and yet so true. And so I felt my heart go out towards one who loved him even better than I— Mary Stringer. There was something terrible in her stoical fortitude. No tear was ever seen in her eyes, no tremor heard in her voice; the only signs she gave of a great grief were silence and immobility of countenance. Day after day she sat by the sick man's bed, with her head and her hands always ready to attend to his wants, keeping every one at a distance by her impenetrable reserve. I used to watch that pale motionless face for hour after hour, until I felt a terrified longing to see it as it looked alone; and one day this came to pass.

Being an artist in a humble way, I had acquired a habit, rather mechanical perhaps, if the truth were told, of noting the shape, colouring, and general effects of any scene before me, and it was one of the poor boy's whims after his fatal accident that I should go up every morning to Farewell Point, and come down and tell him what I had seen; and I went up there for another reason of my own, to have a quiet cry on the spot where all our pleasant talks had taken place, like a silly old woman that I was. Those who fancy that sentimental folly is confined to, or is even peculiar to the young, know very little of human nature.

One warm bright morning I wended my way up to the point with this rational purpose. The sun had not long been up, and had scarcely finished unveiling the calm, oily-looking sea from its night mist shroud; the dew was still dropping from the bright, fresh-looking leaves into the thirsty volcanic soil, and an obstinate *more-pork* was still declaring, in the teeth of all evidence, that the day had not yet commenced, when I gained the summit of the narrow ridge, and there, lying at full length on her face, amongst the luxuriant wild flowers, motionless, except with the convulsive twitching of her fingers, lay—Mary! Frightened, but still more interested, I approached her, but she neither heard nor saw. 'Mary!' said I, gently; and then she started up, with a face that shocked me—haggard, wild, despairing, and above all, defiant.

'I have been a little upset,' said she, slowly, 'but it will pass away directly;' and whilst she spoke the human face seemed to transform itself into marble, as by sheer strength of will she veiled her features once more in their usual blank impenetrable calm.

'I don't want it to pass away like that!' cried I, impulsively, seating myself beside her and drawing her close to me, without noticing whether she was angry or not. 'My poor child, you will kill yourself, or go mad, if you let your sorrow eat into your heart as you do now. Can't you speak out, even to an old woman like me, who loves *him*, in a different way, almost as much as you do?'

My words seemed to soften her, but not in the way they would have softened an ordinary girl. She did not cry; she only said, 'I can't talk,' with a mind of hopeless, bewildered misery, and, laying her head on my shoulder, closed her eyes wearily and was still. And then, after a minute had passed, she raised herself suddenly, scanned my sorrowful face with a wild, eager scrutiny, pressed two or three fierce, passionate kisses on my lips, and rising to her feet, wended her way, erect and alone, down towards the cottage.

And this was the beginning of a friendship— or, rather an affection, for friendship implies some sympathy in character, thought, or opinion—that will last, I firmly believe, till one of us has found rest in death.

A few days after this, as I was strolling towards

the cottage with a bouquet of wild flowers, I noticed a strange boat hauled up on the beach, and on inquiry learnt that it belonged to the Rev. James Brown, of Mahurangi, who was indoors attending to my unfortunate young friend's soul at the very moment. Directly afterwards I met him returning to his boat.

My young friend used laughingly to declare that there were only two breeds of missionary: the lean, brown, dry ones, and the fat, white, damp ones; the Rev. James Brown was of the latter strain. He answered my 'Good morning' by an incoherent exclamation, and went his way gasping and panting, like a wheezy pet spaniel that has just received its first lesson in swimming from some mischievous boy. The simile proved to be not inapt.

As I entered my young friend's room I perceived, by the half-vexed, half-amused smile on his face, that there had been a passage of arms. 'The second of the vultures,' said he, 'has come and gone, having received the dying donkey's last kick. I groaned in spirit when he was announced, for I knew what was coming. He sat himself down by my bed with a kind of gentle moan, and an unctuous leer on his face, intended, I believe, to express a holy pity, that almost tempted me to ask Mary to box his ears. He informed me that he had come to offer me the spiritual consolation of which I stood so much in need. I tried to save him by telling him that our opinions were probably so widely different on such matters that no good could come of our discussing them. But the self-satisfied, well-meaning idiot wouldn't be saved. He said that he had heard of the infidelity of my opinions, but it was not too late for me to leave the paths of error and to return to Divine truth. I told him to remember that from my point of view I was not in error, and moreover could say with an honest conscience that I had sought Divine truth sedulously all my life. He asked me, with pompous dignity, whether he was to understand that I wilfully declined the light that had been graciously revealed.

'" Which particular one of the countless so-called ' revelations ' in the world do you refer to ? " said I.

'" The true one," said he.

'" They each call themselves the true one," replied I, mercilessly.

'" Young man," said he, "you know very well which one I mean ; you are trifling with me."

'" Not the least," replied I. "I merely asked you the question to explain to you that the answer you shall hear directly applies to all of them, and not any one in particular ; " and then I impaled the poor creature on the horns of that terrible humiliating truth that all the world so persistently shuts its eyes to : "As no man can possibly have a prior knowledge of God to enable him to know what God and His thoughts are, no man has a right to say that he is certain that any book, or opinion, or command, or theory, is absolutely God's truth; whence it follows that the truth or untruth of all opinions on supernatural things is a mere question of human judgment and belief; and as no man has a prior knowledge of God to justify him in transforming " I believe " into " I know this is Divine Truth," it follows that you, whether you be a Christian, a Moslem, a Hindu, a Buddhist, a Parsee, or a Fetish-worshipper, have no right whatever to assume that I am wilfully declining Divine truth when I happen to disagree with you about the unknowable."

' The scene that ensued is not easy to describe. He ranted, declaimed, tried to beg the question in every possible way, but I held his mental nose down to the unpalatable truth persistently, administering doses of it in fresh forms whenever he had a lucid interval, till he utterly lost his temper, likened me to an impenitent thief, told me the world I was about to go to (which would have been interesting, had the information been reliable), told me what God's opinions on my way of thinking were (which information had the same defect), and continued with volleys of contradictions and blasphemies till he had made me nearly sick and himself breathless. When he had recovered himself he asked me whether I felt no fear about my future life. I replied, that as I trusted God implicitly I did not. He stared blankly at hearing this, for the fact was, that like many another priest who raves fiercely and continuously from the pulpit against what he calls scepticism, rationalism, or freethinking, he was entirely ignorant of what it really is. I explained to him that men who have not the comforts of what is called revealed light are driven to trust God wholly and blindly; those who find it impossible to do this rush back into some dogmatic creed. But he did not choose to listen to this. He had found that he was a better hand at declamation than argument, and utterly ignoring, with the stern disingenuousness of a polemical theologian, all that had been proved five minutes before, rushed vehemently into the usual attacks upon scepticism, reviling its vain confidence in human reason, its conceit, etc.

'I was getting venomous. "The less you say about conceit," cried I, "the better, considering that the sole difference between us lies in the fact that you consider your human judgment capable of deciding absolutely what theories and impressions are Divine and what are not, while I hold that all such things are beyond the reach of the human intellect. And I do wish that when you religious people of all creeds are abusing the unorthodox, the freethinkers—in short, every one who disagrees with you—you would remember that the men you respect most, the founders of your creeds, were all unorthodox, and to a greater or lesser extent freethinkers."[1]

---

[1] Freethinking does not necessarily lead to Rationalism; for what is meant usually by that term is the offspring of our increased

'At this awful speech he looked as if, like Mrs. Raddles in *Pickwick*, he hoped he mightn't be tempted to forget his sect and strike me; and whilst he stood facing me, opening and shutting his mouth in silence, like some ingenious machine for cutting string, he was seized upon by Mary, and firmly conducted out of the room on the ground that I wasn't to be bothered.'

He made one forget continually that his end was so near; for, living, his spirit had been so thoughtful and earnest that it could scarcely become more so as death approached, while his old love of humour remained the same as ever.

'After all,' said he, after a long pause, 'it was very kind of him to come all this way to try and do me good. I almost wish I had allowed him to think he had converted me. It would have made the worthy creature a proud and happy man, while I—I should have been immortalised in ten thousand tracts. Just think of my humble self contributing to the edification of any number of old ladies, not to speak of their cats.'

'I don't like to hear you speak like that,' said I.

'I am very sorry,' replied he; 'but that well-

scientific knowledge. But a certain amount of free thought, however distorted, has been the cause of every new religion, and each at its birth claims to be more rational, that is to say, more in accordance with man's impressions of all around him, than its predecessor. And in judging this theory, please remember that at the time most of the religions now holding sway in the world were instituted, miracles were looked upon as being no more irrational and improbable than a thunderstorm.

meaning ass's blunders reminded me bitterly how utterly I had wasted my life and its opportunities. I had a noble cause before me, and neglected it, because I thought I might do more harm than good; but I begin to see now that I was mistaken.'

'Do you mean to say,' cried I, astonished, 'that after all you have told me you have come to the conclusion that it was your duty to have set up a pulpit, and to have tried to instil your religion into the world in general?'

'Certainly not,' replied he. 'I am no mad, conceited enthusiast, who fancies that his panacea is going to put the whole world straight, without comparing it calmly and closely with what they already possess, and judging which is likely to suit them best on the whole. My creed is not narrow, exclusive, or conceited enough to be a proselytising one, whether it is likely to do good or the reverse. Looking as I do on all creeds as Divine instruments for the improvement of humanity, I am not likely to try and force down men's throats what is after all only my idea of more perfect truth, unless I am sure it would tend to make men better and happier; and you know that for several reasons I am pretty sure that it would not. Because I have had corns and have been forced to give up shoes, shall I try to force all mankind to do the same, whether they have corns or not? I may, with many others, believe that a time will come when such things will be found unnecessary; but the time is not come, as any one who chooses to study human thought and character may plainly see.

'If I preached a sermon to a mixed assemblage of all classes, religions, and characters, it would be something of this kind: "You who think and you who are frivolous, you whose time and thoughts are devoted to your business in life and you who are idle, you who are educated and you who are not, are met here to-day to hear me speak about my religious creed. I cannot teach it to you, and unless it is already born in your minds I doubt if I can even put you in the way of learning it; but I will try. You will have to devote many years to its study. Begin by travelling until your preconceived ideas about everything are thoroughly shaken. Try to learn meanwhile, at least, the general philosophical truths of science; examine carefully into the creeds of the various races you visit, and compare them with strict impartiality with the one you were brought up in; read a few books on any side of the religious question (if you have any brains it don't matter which), but above all observe and think; make the quest of truth your sole object, and shrink from no conclusions your reason may lead you to; argue on religion with any one who is fool enough to let you, for it is seldom that one man's mind clashes with another's without evolving some spark of new light, and argument makes a man think keenly and explodes fallacies. After a steady course of this kind, together with a mixture of solitude and contemplation of nature and men's minds, you will find your early prejudices considerably weakened ; and to put a finishing touch to them, study such books as *Aids to Faith* and any sermons about freethinking you can get hold of. About this period, if you have not had time and opportunity to become a monomaniac, if you have only read and not thought out things for yourself, if an earnest desire to learn a little of God's greatness is not rooted in your character, you will lapse into reckless despair, sceptical indifference, or violent superstition. If you are really in earnest you will tide over this time, but the more earnest you are the more miserable you will be. Keep on working at the philosophy of science, always remembering that you get nothing from reading without the help of reflection, and that it is the work of your own mind, not that of others, you must depend on. And then perhaps you may arrive at the glorious end that I am honestly proud of ; that is to say, you will have lost all those comforting, helpful dogmas of your old creed that it caused you such misery to leave, you will have gained (if you have escaped shipwreck) a higher, broader idea of Divinity and the universe, and your code of right and wrong will be pretty nearly the same as that you professed before, without the comforting feeling that you used to have, that it represented God's own ideas upon the subject. Now, all you who came here to-day, not because you were dissatisfied with the form of belief you profess, but simply because you were curious to hear some new thing, don't you think you may as well go home again and stick to your old religions, which are more likely to keep you decent than any I can give you the key to? Are you prepared to devote all this time and trouble to the study of a religion which will teach you very little that is new practically, and which, as you are pretty well contented as you are, you can't really want? I have neither the wish nor the power to convert you; but if in the crowd here present there are any earnest sceptics—men who are unable to reconcile their creed with their consciences, I, and others far wiser and cleverer than I, will do our best to help them to work out their own salvation. I shall not attempt to destroy or supplant any portion of your various creeds, except those dogmas which produce intolerance. On that subject I will preach through my whole life." And so ends my imaginary sermon.

'And now you will guess what my purpose in life should have been: to do what little I could towards helping those floundering in the sea of thought like myself; and, as far as the world in general is concerned, to contribute my mite towards the suppression of intolerance in all creeds.

'The only way in which this can ever be done is by teaching mankind the mental foundations on which their belief is founded, and forcing them to see what the things they abuse really are. For as surely as conceit is the mother of intolerance, ignorance is the father. All the misery, the bitterness, the sorrow, the loneliness produced in so many families that I know by religious difference, have their real root in ignorance. For instance, a religious family look upon a sceptic amongst them as something wicked and horrible, simply because they don't know the mental grounds of their own belief or the nature of his. Every Sunday, in many a pulpit, an imaginary freethinker—a distorted, foolish, lying caricature—is stuck up, and of course triumphantly knocked down again, with the whole question begged; while we sceptics, fools that we are, smile at the preacher's ignorance or growl at his disingenuousness, seldom reflecting that the promulgation of such misstatements and slanders is the cause of the bitter loneliness of our lives. Unless we speak out plainly and fairly, how is this mass of lying and misconception to be cleared away?

'I tell you that if I could have persuaded half a dozen religious men that scepticism is born, not out of conceit in human judgment, but the reverse: not out of indifference, but earnestness—not out of irreverence, but reverence for God—that far from being a vain glorification of the human intellect, it claimed a narrower limit for its powers; if I could have shown them the real grounds on which it differed from religion—convinced them that the responsibility of what we believe or disbelieve *must* rest upon our private human judgment, and that therefore we should look upon differences in religion merely as differences in opinion and fallacies of thought—I should feel that I had done my duty in my generation. The only way men can become tolerant is by learning the roots, first of their own opinions, then of those that disagree.'

'But haven't you always told me,' said I, 'that what you called "intolerance," "exclusiveness," "narrowness," "conceit," in religious thought, had a power for good over men's actions that seemed to balance its evils?'

'It is a great problem,' replied he, slowly. 'Complete intolerance means fanatical persecution; complete tolerance (utterly impossible to men as they are) would mean indifference. We must strike a medium as well as we can—a medium that will change perpetually as men change. Intolerance produced by a narrow exclusive view of Divine favours seemed, to the best of my knowledge, to be intrinsically wrong, and my scruples in attacking it were very absurd; something like a child hesitating to pull off a piece of bark from a tree for fear it should bring the tree down with a crash. I begin to think that without knowing it I have been a conceited fool. I can only say that I acted according to my lights.

'But even if I could not have rid myself of the habit of looking at everything from both sides of the hedge, I should have made public my very hesitation and its reasons. For there is a kind of good, but utterly illogical, tolerance gaining ground amongst mankind, the roots of which require to be exposed, by showing the principles, the virtues, and the vices of both tolerance and intolerance. It is a confused feeling, more of the heart than the head, amongst those who unconsciously drop out of sight the exclusive and damnatory tenets of their creeds. And unless this movement is looked fairly in the face, unless religious tenets about God are made to keep pace with the development of the human mind, there will come a time (I have seen signs of it already) when a great mass of men will be startled to find themselves positive disbelievers in the actual meaning of the dogmas they profess, and will rush into infidelity, not because they are fit to accept a natural religion void of dogma and superstition, but because they have outgrown some of the articles of their creeds. The consequence of this anarchy of thought will be to purify religions, but the process will be dreadful—violent alternations between reckless atheism and frantic superstition.'

'I don't quite see,' said I, after a long pause, 'how you can reconcile the two purposes, of obtaining toleration by showing what scepticism really is, and of trying to give help and sympathy to sceptics, with your determination not to preach your own religion.'

'It all depends upon what you mean by preaching,' replied he. 'You would not suspect a man who wrote an article in the *Quarterly*, showing fairly what Mohammedanism was, and how it differed from Christianity, of trying to convert people to the faith of Mohammed. What *I* understand by preaching a religion is trying by every possible means to convert people from their faith to yours, trying to show your faith in the most attractive light and to hide its practical deficiencies. If you will think over our various conversations, you will not accuse me of *that*. Besides, this scepticism has (at any rate apparently) none of the comforts for which men value their religions. It has no attraction whatever, but the reverse. And men who have a religion that contents them may be converted to another faith by their feelings and inclinations, but never by simple reason, to a way of thinking whose sole glory is a painful, humble uncertainty on subjects they could scarcely bear to doubt upon for a moment. I am past the folly of thinking that I either would or *could* influence such men towards anything except a little wider toleration.

'But to those who are not content—those who, either from the greater earnestness, originality, or sensitiveness of their minds, or from having the sleep of early prejudice destroyed by various causes, feel the vivid common-sense reality of many things which to others convey no startling meaning—those to whom many of the doctrines of the creed they were brought up in seem perpetual offences against God and their conscience, I would cry: Work out your own salvation! I honestly believe it is their best path; for if they do not cast the offending dogmas away and seek truth by honest, fearless thought, they either benumb themselves into a terrible indifference, or, having forced themselves to believe in the tenets that caused them such misery, they produce a ghastly caricature of their creed, with all its worst points fanatically exaggerated, which shocks and astonishes their fellow-believers, who have not experienced the phases of mind they have passed through.

'You will say that the experiment is a dangerous one. I will not deny it. The man accustomed to support life on stimulants and narcotics may find a sudden change to a simple diet unpleasant, perhaps fatal. But it saves them at least from the terrible spirit death, or the no less terrible distortion of mind that I have just spoken of. And I think the danger is somewhat overdrawn. The man whose faith in the religion of his birth is shaken only by the love of truth and reverence for God, is not likely to rush despairingly to lower things in his search for a haven.'

'Yes,' continued he, dreamily, 'there *is* a haven, once we have passed through the bitter ordeal of finding some knowledge beyond our reach that we had been taught to think so near.

'If we can find peace for our consciences in no dogmatic creed we have God left to us, with all His universe, as the book to teach us a little of His ways. Every new discovery in science adds to our feeling of His omnipresent wonder, and places another stone in the walls of a temple of pure Monotheism.

'It was not always thus, and we should be thankful that we live as late as we do. There was a time when a man who, even from a spirit of reverence, doubted the religion of his day, had no refuge for his soul to flee to. Nature could then give him but little help; the foolish doctrine of entities was then in existence, and the false charge of Atheism, levelled to this day against free thought and infidelity, was then true. But science has done and is doing the great work. Stretching out its researches in all directions, showing the inscrutable mystery of all things, small and great, it is teaching us a universal God, unconfined within the pale of any human creed, and forcing us to believe in Him and trust Him.

'The old blank hopelessness of the earnest sceptic is passing away. When his faith in the theory he has been brought up in has broken down, he does not feel that God has gone with it. All around him testifies to Him, and he has now a power of realising the greatness and the marvel of His works, and of learning from that realisation an implicit trust in Him, that in a past age could scarcely have been more than a misty dream. Out of a bitter lesson of humility come first trust and then peace.'

He seemed exhausted and inclined to sleep, so I left him and went home.

Three days afterwards, as I was returning from my usual pilgrimage to Farewell Point, I met Dan seeking me, with his message written in his face. 'It is coming,' whispered he; and I followed him in silence to the cottage.

As I entered the room I saw Mary kneeling by the bedside, with her face buried in the pillow. I bent over the dying boy and kissed him, for I could not speak. He took my hand and laid it gently on Mary's head. She looked up, and he, touching her forehead with his lips, settled his face in the pillow, like a weary child falling asleep, and was still.

.   .   .   .   .

'What is the object,' may be asked, 'of giving this eccentric young man's thoughts and opinions? Who can be any the better for reading them?'

In the first place, let me say that this eccentric boy's mind is a type of a class among the most earnest and thoughtful young men of the day— far more common than is usually supposed, because, for obvious reasons, they keep their opinions secret from all but their fellow-sufferers.

My first object is, by showing what a sceptic really is when stripped of the slanders constantly hurled against him, to plead to society in general for a little more fairness and toleration towards him; for though the strength and purity of my young friend's individual character held him up, I *know* of many of his way of thinking who have been driven into morbid vanity, indifference, and despair, entirely by the narrow, ignorant want of charity of the people about them. I almost doubt sometimes whether the good people of this world have not ruined as many souls as the wicked!

But I have another object: to teach (if possible) a lesson by example to young freethinkers themselves. For there is another class of earnest sceptics far more noisy, if not more numerous, I grieve to say, than that represented by my young friend, who, though bearing a general likeness to him in their general method of thought, are widely different from him in several very important particulars. On entering manhood, their second birth, their period of *Sturm und Drang*, as my poor boy used to call it, comes suddenly upon them. They become positively intoxicated all at once by the superb logic of the philosophical writers of the day; and their conversion is generally extreme, because it is sudden—shallow, because it has been developed more by quick external than gradual internal means. In religion and politics they are equally radical; they are as bigoted as the opponents they hate and despise most, for they cannot acknowledge the good worked by any belief but their own. Both in religion and politics they would destroy, if they had the power, everything that does not fit itself to their ideas, without reflecting whether it does most harm or most good, or whether they have anything equally serviceable to replace it; and they will boldly defend this line of conduct by saying, 'It is not our business to calculate about the utility of anything: the question is one of right or wrong. Has not the greatest thinker of our day proved conclusively that we should be guided only by what is right according to first principles, because no man can have a sufficient knowledge of other minds to justify him in neglecting abstract right for what he considers utility? Read *Social Statics*, etc., and they will teach you the *truth*, dear Mrs. ——, as they have done me.' Oh, pot and kettle! pot and kettle! as my young friend would have said. Both these young fanatics, and often the idols they worship, seem to forget entirely that men disagree as utterly about the rectitude as they do about the utility of all things—religious, political, and social; and, moreover, that no two of their idolised philosophers, starting from the same first principle, arrive on the whole at the same conclusions. To my young friend's serious question, 'Supposing that all the superstitions, the false claims to Divine knowledge, which exist now, could be abolished, what could you put in their places which would have an equal power for good over the actions of mankind?' They have only the fanatical argument above quoted to answer with; a sophism which, a little caricatured, seems to be: 'You are utterly to discard your fallible knowledge of what is likely to do good, and to look on your opinion of what is abstract truth as infallible.' The fact is, that this school manage, like their religious opponents, though in a different way, to look upon abstract truth and utility as identical, which, *when men are perfected*, they no doubt will be. To explain. The religious man says, 'See, how useful this dogma is in improving mankind ; *therefore* it must be true.' The other says, 'See, how incontestably true this conclusion is ; *therefore* it *must* have a power for good over men's minds.' My young friend would have said, 'Both inferences are equally unjustifiable. Men being perfect, it is possible that absolute truth and what is best for them may be identical ; but men being imperfect, an opinion may be too much before the age to be beneficial if spread, just as we see many opinions once useful now behind it ; so, until we near the goal of perfection, we must remember that absolute truth and utility cannot be identical, and that, moreover, we have no right to claim a knowledge of what absolute truth is. The essence, the glory, of the sceptic's creed should be the humility that is born of doubt—the doubt that is born of a broad, wide power of acknowledging that all things equally are part of God's work. Directly we begin to claim absolute truth we become as bad as the bigots we despise ; nay, worse ; for they have been brought up to believe their creed an incontestable truth, and our training should have taught us more liberality.' Whether my young friend's mind was one to be admired or despised, I leave it to my readers to decide.

STANDARD WORKS FOR THE LIBRARY.

PROFESSOR MOMMSEN'S HISTORY OF ROME TO THE TIME OF AUGUSTUS. Translated by Dr. DICKSON. LIBRARY EDITION, in 4 vols., demy 8vo, 75s. The POPULAR EDITION, in 4 vols., crown 8vo, 46s. 6d.
** This last Edition is sold in certain Volumes separately; also Vols. I. and II., 21s.; Vol. III., 10s. 6d.; Vol. IV., 15s.

THE ROMAN PROVINCES. Being the History of Rome from Cæsar to Diocletian. By Professor MOMMSEN. Translated by Rev. P. W. DICKSON. 2 vols., 8vo, 36s.

THE HISTORY OF ANTIQUITY. From the German of Professor MAX DUNCKER. By EVELYN ABBOTT, M.A., LL.D., of Balliol College, Oxford. In 6 vols., demy 8vo. Each volume can be obtained separately, 21s.

ESSAYS: Classical and Theological. By CONNOP THIRLWALL, D.D., late Bishop of St. David's. Demy 8vo, 15s.

THE CHURCH AND ITS ORDINANCES. By the late Dean HOOK. 2 vols., demy 8vo, 10s. 6d.

THE LIVES OF THE ARCHBISHOPS OF CANTERBURY. By WALTER FARQUHAR HOOK, late Dean of Chichester. ST. AUGUSTINE to JUXON. 12 vols., demy 8vo, £9. Each separately (with exception of III., IV., VI., and VII.), 15s. The New Series begins with Vol. VI. Vol. XII. is the Index.

THE HEAVENS. By AMÉDÉE GUILLEMIN. In demy 8vo, with over Two Hundred Illustrations, 12s.

THE HISTORY OF THE THIRTY YEARS' WAR. From the German of ANTON GINDELY. In 2 vols., large crown 8vo, with Maps and Illustrations, 24s.

THE LETTERS OF HORACE WALPOLE, FOURTH EARL OF ORFORD. Edited by PETER CUNNINGHAM. In 9 vols., demy 8vo, with Portraits, 94s. 6d.

THE HISTORY OF THE GREAT FRENCH REVOLUTION. From the French of M. THIERS. By FREDERICK SHOBERL. With Forty-one fine Engravings, and Portraits of the most Celebrated Personages referred to in the Work, engraved on Steel by WILLIAM GREATBACH. 5 vols., demy 8vo, 36s.

THE FIFTEEN DECISIVE BATTLES OF THE WORLD. By Professor CREASY. LIBRARY EDITION, in demy 8vo, 10s. 6d.

MEMOIRS OF NAPOLEON BONAPARTE. By FAUVELET DE BOURRIENNE, Private Secretary to the Emperor. Edited by Colonel PHIPPS. 3 vols., demy 8vo. Map and Thirty-eight fine Illustrations on Steel, 42s.

THE NAVAL HISTORY OF GREAT BRITAIN. By WILLIAM JAMES. In 6 vols., crown 8vo, with Portraits of Distinguished Commanders, on Steel, 42s.

RICHARD BENTLEY & SON, NEW BURLINGTON ST., LONDON.

www.ingramcontent.com/pod-product-compliance
Lightning Source LLC
Chambersburg PA
CBHW031438160426
43195CB00010BB/779